D0801517

# GENDER INEQUALITY IN SPORTS

## FROM TITLE IX TO WORLD TITLES

KIRSTIN CRONN-MILLS

TWENTY-FIRST CENTURY BOOKS / MINNEAPOLIS

# THIS BOOK IS FOR ALL THE GIRLS AND WOMEN WHO LOVE SPORTS AND PLAY EXACTLY LIKE A GIRL, WITH NO APOLOGY.

Twenty-First Century Books™
An imprint of Lerner Publishing Group, Inc.
241 First Avenue North
Minneapolis, MN 55401 USA

For reading levels and more information, look up this title at www.lernerbooks.com.

Main body text set in Adobe Garamond Pro.
Typeface provided by Adobe Inc.

**Library of Congress Cataloging-in-Publication Data**

Names: Cronn-Mills, Kirstin, 1968– author.
Title: Gender inequality in sports: from Title IX to world titles / Kirstin Cronn-Mills.
Description: Minneapolis: Twenty-First Century Books, [2022] | Includes bibliographical references and index. | Audience: Ages 13–18 years | Audience: Grades 7–9 | Summary: "A comprehensive view of gender inequality in sports, this book details the continued struggle against unequal pay, discrimination, and sexism despite the landmark law of Title IX"—Provided by publisher.
Identifiers: LCCN 2021033647 (print) | LCCN 2021033648 (ebook) | ISBN 9781728419473 (Library Binding) | ISBN 9781728445410 (eBook)
Subjects: LCSH: United States. Education Amendments of 1972. Title IX—History. | Sports for women—United States—History. | Sex discrimination in sports—United States—History. | Sports for women—Law and legislation—United States—History. | Sex discrimination in sports—Law and legislation—United States—History.
Classification: LCC GV709.18.U6 C76 2022 (print) | LCC GV709.18.U6 (ebook) | DDC 796.082—dc23

LC record available at https://lccn.loc.gov/2021033647
LC ebook record available at https://lccn.loc.gov/2021033648

Manufactured in the United States of America
1-49070-49268-11/19/2021

# CONTENTS

# CHAPTER 1

# Why Not Equality?

S it down on the bench of a ten-year-old girls' soccer team. Ask them if teams like theirs have always been part of soccer leagues. DUH. Their faces will show you how dumb that question is. Of course girls' soccer teams have always existed! Move from the bench to the sidelines to ask the girls' grandmothers and great-grandmothers. They'll probably give you a different answer.

Why should we care that girls play sports? Why should people play sports at all? Sports are fun, they can keep us healthy, they teach us how to work together, and they provide transferable skills to careers. According to a 2016 survey of four hundred women executives on four continents, 96 percent of them played a sport. These same executives said their time in sports developed these three leadership qualities: the ability to finish projects, motivational skills, and team-building skills.

However, women's sports history is very different from men's. It may be difficult to imagine that female athletes struggled to be allowed on the field—but they did. That fight shifted when Title IX, part of the Education Amendments of 1972, created a federal law barring discrimination based on sex in all federally funded education programs. Even though sports isn't mentioned in the law, Title IX was a primary driver for creating sports opportunities for women, in both K–12 and college. In 1971, before the law, women athletes were 7.4 percent of varsity athletes in high schools. Thirty-five years later, in 2007, they were 41 percent of high school varsity athletes.

Women's amateur and professional sports have also grown, due to Title IX, because of the increase in female athletes and sports teams for women and girls. Women's sports outside of schools isn't governed by Title IX, but Title IX legislation caused many more women to make their sport their career. Because tennis legend Billie Jean King understood the impact the law would have on professional women's sports, she testified before Congress in 1972, promoting its passage.

Even with Title IX and all the growth in women's sports, we still don't have many women sports decision makers at the highest levels. The International Olympic Committee (founded in 1894) hasn't had a woman leader. Neither has FIFA (the International Federation of Association Football, founded in 1904). The latter is the international governing body for football (called soccer in the US). Sarah Hirshland became the first female CEO of the US Olympic and Paralympic Committee in 2018, forty-six years after Title IX.

Despite the fights for equity and equality over the last fifty years, men's sports and male athletes still have considerable advantages over women's sports and female athletes. This book will help you

# SARAH FULLER, SOCCER AND FOOTBALL PLAYER, AND HER PREDECESSORS

In the fall of 2020, Sarah Fuller was the goalkeeper for the women's Southeast Conference championship soccer team at Vanderbilt University. When Vanderbilt's football team had its kickers sidelined due to COVID-19, then football coach Derek Mason turned to Fuller to replace them. Though soccer players have been called on to handle kicking duties for football teams in both high school and college, Vanderbilt doesn't have a men's soccer team to call on. Fuller knew her presence on the football field would be historic: "I just think it's incredible that I am able to do this, and all I want to do is be a good influence to the young girls out there."

Fuller then became the first woman to kick in a Power Five conference—the elite conferences in college football—in Vanderbilt's game on November 28, 2020. For that kick, she was named the Southeastern Conference Co-Special Teams Player of the Week. She then became the first woman to score in a Power Five football game on December 12, 2020, when she kicked two different extra points after touchdowns.

Fuller kicked off the second half of the Vanderbilt-Missouri game on November 28, 2020, and became the first woman to play in a Southeastern Conference football game.

Fuller is the third woman to play in the Football Bowl Subdivision of the Division I National Collegiate Athletic Association (NCAA). In 2003 Katie Hnida kicked two extra points for the University of New Mexico. In 2015 April Goss kicked an extra point for Kent State University.

During her tenure on the US Olympic and Paralympic Committee, Hirshland oversaw reforms focused on athlete wellness, including safety measures and increased access to medical and mental health treatment.

see why those disparities exist and why they're perpetuated. Title IX has helped us get closer to equity and equality. But we still have a long way to go before sports equality applies to children in elementary school sports and world champion athletes alike.

Equality is, of course, the goal for men's and women's sports. This book uses the word *inequality* in its title because it's the word most people think of first when they search for the imbalance of power between men and women. But more than equality is at stake. Men and women need *equitable* sports opportunities, so this book is also about *inequity*. *Equality* means "all individuals receive the same things." *Equity* means "meeting people's needs in the pursuit of making sure individuals are equal." We need both equity and equality in women's sports in the US.

Despite these equity and equality fights, a general disregard for women in sports still exists. Here are a couple of examples, but there are many more:

- Former Louisiana State University head football coach Les Miles was banned from having one-on-one contact with female student employees, after he was accused of kissing one and texting her and another student from his personal phone. He also requested that student employees be "attractive, blonde, and fit." The ban happened in 2013, and Miles left LSU in 2016. He received no other sanction for his harassment, though the athletic director recommended he be fired. When this news broke in March 2021, he was placed on administrative leave and then fired from Kansas University, where he'd been hired as the head football coach in 2018.

- Streaming service Disney+ released a show in April 2021 called *Big Shot*. The show stars John Stamos, and Stamos said, "I play a hot headed basketball coach who gets kicked out of the NCAA. On his road to redemption, he is forced to coach at an all girls private high school in Laguna." The poster for the show shows Stamos surrounded by two adult women and five girls. One of the women is Black, and at least three of the girls are girls of color.

Sports writer Lindsay Gibbs says, "Disney is really using a girls' basketball team, made up primarily of girls of color, to tell the story of a white man. Disney is really treating women's sports as punishment. Disney is really pushing a redemption arc on a 'hot headed' (read: abusive) coach. Disney is really using WOMEN'S SPORTS as the setting for a white man's redemption story. WHOSE IDEA WAS THIS?"

## WHAT ARE SEXISM AND FEMINISM?

A web search for the word *sexism* offers many definitions, but basically, sexism is prejudice or discrimination based on gender. Though the definition applies to people of any gender, sexism usually means men are valued more than women—and given more power, based on that value. For this book, the power of sexism means sports decision makers (team owners, athletic directors, powerful players, media, and fans) value men's sports, players, and coaches more than they value women's sports, players, and coaches.

Sexism affects and harms all humans, not just women. Men are harmed by sexism because it sets a narrow boundary for men's thoughts and behaviors, and it often asks men to devalue women to be "one of the guys." One of the worst insults a male athlete could hear? "You play like a girl." If being like a girl or woman is an insult (implying less strength, usually), why would we think girls' or women's sports would be valued?

In the United States, and many countries around the world, sexism is systemic—it affects all parts of our lives. Women and girls often report being devalued in medicine, education, the workforce, and domestic life.

# ANTOINETTE (TONI) HARRIS AND HER FOOTBALL SCHOLARSHIP

Toni Harris fell in love with football when she was five. She played junior varsity football at her high school, Redford Union High School, in suburban Detroit, Michigan. At the University of Toledo, she intended to walk on with the team. Her plans were interrupted by ovarian cancer. Once she won that battle (after losing 80 pounds, or 36 kg, and struggling with harsh chemo), she reenrolled in college at East Los Angeles College. There, she convinced football coach Bobby Godinez to let her play as a wide receiver and cornerback. She played three games with them. Then she sent a tape of her highlights to over two hundred four-year schools, hoping to find a program. Footage of her was used in a Super Bowl commercial for Toyota during Super Bowl LIII on February 3, 2019.

She chose to play for Central Methodist University in Fayette, Missouri, under coach David Calloway. Harris is the first woman, and first Black woman, to play a skills position in college football on a scholarship.

In 2019, Harris told an interviewer that she was aiming to be the first woman player in the National Football League (NFL). "If it doesn't happen, I can just pave the way for another little girl to come out and play, or even start a women's NFL," she said.

Title IX was one of the remedies created for this devaluation. In 1972, before Title IX was passed, women earned 7 percent of law degrees and 9 percent of medical degrees. Law schools and medical schools receive federal funding, so after 1972, they were subject to Title IX regulations and parity standards. Thirty-five years later, in 2007, women graduated with 47.5 percent of law degrees and 49.1 percent of medical degrees.

Sexism could be fixed if men would demand equal treatment for everyone, as women generally do. Because of sexism and our *patriarchy* (a society that privileges the power of men), men hold the power to make the change. If men's players, coaches, leagues, team owners, and governing bodies would commit to the equity and equality of women's sports, eliminating sexism would be achievable.

*Feminism* isn't a negative word, nor is it an exclusionary word. Feminism is the desire to have all genders treated equally and provided with the same opportunities in all areas of society. Feminism supports people's right to choose their jobs and roles in life, especially if those choices go against gender

## TRAILBLAZING WOMEN ATHLETES: ALTHEA GIBSON AND WILMA RUDOLPH

Before we had Serena and Venus, before Simone, Suni, and Naomi, we had Althea Gibson and Wilma Rudolph. Though they came before the era of megastar athletes, Gibson and Rudolph set the stage for the powerhouse women athletes of color who came after them.

Tennis player Althea Gibson cracked the color barrier in both tennis and golf. Born in 1927 in South Carolina, she was the first Black player to win a Grand Slam title (the 1956 French Championships), and she then went on to win both Wimbledon and the US Nationals in 1957 and 1958. She was voted the Female stereotypes, such as stay-at-home dads and women welders. According to ThoughtCo.com, "The history of feminism is simply the history of women striving to experience their full humanity in a world shaped by and for men." Feminism has a long history in the United States, though it has often excluded non-white women, women with disabilities, and LGBTQIA+ women—a mistake many twenty-first-century feminists strive to correct.

Feminism is useful to sports because it advocates for equity and equality for women and men. It wants women to compete in clothes that are comfortable and useful for their sport—not clothes that are meant to be sexy and cute. Feminism wants all athletes to be paid equally for their labor and entertainment value. Feminism wants women's sports to have air time and wide advertising campaigns, so more people can see their sports.

## WHY WAS TITLE IX CREATED?

Even though they most likely don't know their sports history, those young soccer players most likely *do* understand that gap in respect

Athlete of the Year in both of those years by the Associated Press. When she switched her attention to golf, she was the first Black woman to play on the Women's Professional Golf Tour.

Black runner Wilma Rudolph was born in Tennessee in 1940. She had both polio and scarlet fever as a young child, resulting in her need for a leg brace. Her large family helped her rehabilitate her leg, and by high school, she was nominated as an All-American athlete in basketball. However, her passion was running. She won a bronze medal in the 1956 Olympic 4x100 relay, and she brought home three gold medals from the 1960 Olympics, after breaking three world records. She was voted the Female Athlete of the Year in 1961 by the Associated Press.

levels for men's and women's sports. Those young players might be able to identify that girls and women's sports aren't valued the same as men's teams, because it's what they've been shown by our culture. This book asks why that disparity exists and what we can do to shift the balance of power to make things more equitable.

Title IX was created to address inequality and inequity in federally funded programs, including sports. What created the need to address the

## MELINA LOBITZ, HIGH SCHOOL AND COLLEGE ATHLETE

Melina Lobitz, a midwestern athlete at a Division I university, talks about how women's and men's teams are treated:

High school was cool because our men's soccer team sucked, so we were THE soccer team [at our mid-sized high school]. We were very fortunate because if you wanted to watch soccer, you had to watch us. The girls' hockey and basketball teams didn't get that attention.

When we were rowing [at college], we all knew that the entire reason we were able to be D1 athletes instead of club athletes (the men's team is club rowing) was Title IX, and that they have to balance out for men's teams. So we had access to the athlete's dining and athletic facilities, but we were there to balance the men. Whether it's because we were rowing, or because we were women, we were a non-factor in the college's sports world.

The arena where the men play hockey at my college is huge. The arena where the women play is connected to inequality? The disparity was generated by forces we have in the United States that keep resources unequal, including racism, sexism, homophobia, and other forms of discrimination. Sexism is the force that drives legislation like Title IX, but this book will also address racism, homophobia, and transphobia, because they figure into the expansion of Title IX's protections.

The sports world operates in a binary system when it comes to gender. But some athletes don't fit into the binary genders of men and

the men's arena, but the capacity for seating is a third to half the size of the men's arena. They could literally switch men's and women's games in the big arena, but of course they don't. And the women have been ranked first in D1 hockey. We've won big tournaments almost every year since 2014, and conference championships as well. We're plenty good. We were NCAA champions, too. But women still have the smaller hockey arena.

If we want women's sports to be equitable with men's, we have to give people access to women's teams. We have to put them on TV and give them visibility. It's so hard to watch the National Women's Soccer League games—why? The only way I can follow them is on Twitter. Why isn't ESPN reporting their scores, too? A lot of our women's national players are signed over in the UK, with their women's Premiere League. I can't find their scores! Why? It's not that hard.

In political debates, you have to give equal time to each side. Why isn't that true for women's sports? They do the same things in the same season. Why aren't they at least included in the ticker at the bottom of ESPN? Why do we have to say "basketball" and "women's basketball"?

women. While this book will generally refer to men/male and women/female athletes, some athletes identify as non-binary (Canadian soccer player Quinn, WNBA player Layshia Clarendon, and Olympic skateboarder Alana Smith, for example) and transgender, though many trans athletes are part of the gender binary. No matter what an athlete's gender identity is, they are still entitled to equity and equality, in high school, college, or beyond.

Mori resigned from the Tokyo Olympic organizing committee following public outcry. However, he defended his statement and argued that he was unfairly criticized because of his age.

Remember those young soccer players on their bench? They may be able to give you the name of some famous women soccer players and coaches—such as Jill Ellis, Megan Rapinoe, and Alex Morgan. But they could have trouble naming any teams from the National Women's Soccer League. They could be unaware of its existence, since teams didn't begin play until 2013 (men's Major League Soccer began in 1993 in the US). If they know it exists, they might tell you they don't get to watch any games on TV, because networks won't show them.

Why would young girls have so little information about the professional part of their sport? Some girls on the team might not be interested in anything more than having fun, but some girls might have dreams of high school, college, and professional play. Why aren't those girls easily able to see role models for those dreams?

The ultimate question is, Why don't we value women in sports?

Title IX remains one of the few bridges to equity and equality for women in the United States—and it's in a very limited arena. On Billie Jean King's website, she reminds us that "Title IX remains the only law that grants women any kind of equality in America."

Why is there only one law?

The fight for equity and equality must continue or the disrespect will carry on. In early February 2021, Tokyo was preparing to host the postponed 2020 Summer Olympics. Yoshiro Mori, president of the Tokyo Olympics organizing committee, said that any women added to the committee must learn to speak

## THE LENS OF RACE IN SPORTS AND IN AMERICA

Americans have a complex relationship with race. No matter the color of our skin, we're always looking at events and individuals through a racial lens—it affects how we see, hear, feel, and understand the world around us. If we're white, we must be as conscious of race as people who are not white.

Racial stereotypes are part of the sports world. They're woven into how we talk about players (white players as "crafty" and Black players as "sneaky"), and how tall Black men are automatically assumed to be basketball players, when they might be bank presidents or teachers. We seem to mention the color of someone's skin only if they're non-white: the football player and the Black football player. We must understand that whiteness isn't a "default setting" for sports, American culture, or anything else.

In this book, we could mention the skin color or culture of every athlete we singled out, or we could choose to mention a person's skin color or culture only if it's relevant to the story in the book. We chose the latter approach, but our stance is this: race matters, and race complicates sport, just as race complicates the United States. We must be honest about its inclusion in our lives.

briefly because women speak too much in meetings. Nobody in the meeting stepped in to defend women. The backlash was swift. Many Olympic volunteers resigned to protest Mori's remarks, and the public complained to the Japanese organizers. Corporate sponsors of the Olympics were worried about what other remarks Mori would make. Mori resigned on February 12, 2021. He acknowledged his remarks had caused controversy, but he didn't agree that his comment demeaned women. The problems, he said, were with the interpretation of the remarks.

Also in February 2021, Senator Rand Paul of Kentucky repeatedly misgendered trans girls in sports during a confirmation hearing with Secretary of Education Miguel Cardona. Paul referred to trans girls as boys and said the concept of letting transgender girls compete in girls' sports was "bizarre." Paul wondered if "boys" competing with girls would ruin women's athletics. Cardona said that schools have responsibilities to provide opportunities for all kids, including transgender kids, to participate in activities like sports.

This book will help you understand more about inequality in women's sports and how Title IX has helped the fight for equity and equality. It will also provide ideas for what we might do to ramp up the fight for equity and equality for girls' and women's sports in America. All athletes deserve the same opportunities. This book will show you why that doesn't happen in the United States, and what we can do about it.

Remember that change in the sports world can be lightning fast or glacially slow, but change will continue. As you read this book, you may recognize many differences in women's sports since its publication—or there may be very few. It's hard to predict. Hopefully, the progress of women's equity and equality will continue to gain speed in the twenty-first century. If this book doesn't mention your favorite female athlete, maybe you could write her story so other students have access to it.

# INTERSECTIONALITY
# AND SERENA WILLIAMS

When we talk about women, in sports or anywhere else, we have to talk about how race, sexuality, or any other part of their identity affects the sexism they face. It's especially true when women are criticized, including athletes. All of the -phobias and -isms women face can work together to hold them down. *Intersectionality* is a framework created by Black feminist scholar and law professor Kimberlé Williams Crenshaw in 1989. It's a way to analyze how our social and political identities come together to create or amplify both discrimination and privilege. For example, if you're a woman and you're Black, you may experience amplified discrimination due to the combination of your identities.

When President Joe Biden created his executive order reinforcing antidiscrimination under Title IX on his first day in office in January 2021, he also included intersectionality: "Discrimination on the basis of gender identity or sexual orientation manifests differently for different individuals, and it often overlaps with other forms of prohibited discrimination, including discrimination on the basis of race or disability. For example, transgender Black Americans face unconscionably high levels of workplace discrimination, homelessness, and violence, including fatal violence." Biden is the first US president to mention intersectionality in an executive order.

Intersectionality matters in the sports world. Elite tennis player Serena Williams—the most successful women's tennis player in American sports, with seventy-three career titles, including twenty-three Grand Slam singles titles, plus career earnings of over $95 million—is often criticized for bringing "drama" to the court by displaying her emotions. If she questions an umpire's call during a tennis match, she is chastised for that

Williams (*right*) argues with chair umpire Carlos Ramos during the 2018 US Open.

display in ways famously emotional male tennis players like John McEnroe, Andre Agassi, and Roger Federer, are not. In the 2021 Australian Open, former tennis champion Chris Evert criticized Williams for her emotions during Williams's loss to tennis star Naomi Osaka. The backlash for Evert's commentary was swift. Tennis fans pointed out it wasn't the first time Evert had been critical of Williams for similar reasons. On Twitter, tennis fan Mythri Jegathesan criticized Evert as the face of "misogynoir," a term coined by writer Moya Bailey to indicate a special kind of criticism reserved for Black (noir) women (misogyny).

Professor Crystal Fleming used this same word when she wrote about Williams's argument with a chair umpire at the 2018 US Open, which produced a fine for Williams. Williams called the umpire a "thief," claiming he stole a point from her.

After the match, John McEnroe noted he'd said much worse to chair umpires without a fine. Fleming was present at the match and witnessed the confrontation over unfair calls. Fleming's evaluation was clear: "The unfair expectations [of keeping her emotions in check] imposed on Williams represent misogynoir—a concoction of racialized sexism that targets black women. It's clear that the mistreatment she experienced during the match was a lesson in multiple forms of discrimination and oppression that [B]lack women routinely face."

Professor Treva Lindsey agrees that pointing out Williams's emotional outbursts is both racist and sexist: "It's another way of framing this long-standing stereotype of the angry Black woman. . . . Specifically, Black women are framed as irrationally angry and therefore aggressive, and therefore bringing unnecessary drama to their workplace, too."

Serena Williams isn't the only Black female athlete for whom intersectionality creates frustrating barriers. She's just one of the most prominent. When sexism combines with racism, homophobia, ableism, or a combination of these, women athletes face enormous barriers to equity and equality.

**Williams plays against Aliaksandra Sasnovich in the first round of the ladies' singles match of Wimbledon 2021.**

# CHAPTER 2

# Title IX and Its Evolution

The progress of women's sports across the globe has been quite slow. Women competed in the Heraean Games, held in Ancient Greece in the sixth century BCE. Cynisca (born ca. 440 BCE), a daughter of a Spartan king, won the four-horse chariot race in 396 and 392. She was considered the first female Olympian. Daughters of wealthy Romans were also able to compete in men's sporting competitions.

Not much is recorded about women's sports after the ancient world. Leisure activities such as sports were only available to wealthy individuals who had time for such things. Mary Queen of Scots is considered the first known female golfer, taking to the greens in 1552, but she is one of the few women we know of who participated in sports. Other wealthy women may also have been active in events deemed "ladylike" enough to preserve women's modesty and dignity. Up through the mid-1800s, women weren't encouraged to exert themselves (and prevailing thought said that humans had a finite amount of energy, so conservation was important).

By the late 1800s, women started to form sports clubs in urban areas to enjoy some competition. In 1893 New York golf

Mary, Queen of Scots was well known for her golfing prowess but was also talented in hunting, horseback riding, and archery.

club Shinnecock Hills created a nine-hole course especially for women, and offered memberships to them as well. Early college sports for women were mostly intramural (competitions between students), though Smith College, a women's college, had a basketball team in 1892. Soon after other women's colleges had basketball teams. The first college basketball teams competed against each other in 1896, in California and Washington. A tennis match was played between Bryn Mawr and Vassar, both women's colleges at the time, but it was canceled because Vassar didn't want to allow women to compete. Women began competing at the Olympics Games in Paris in 1900—but just barely. Out of almost a thousand athletes, only twenty-two were women. They were allowed to compete in tennis, sailing, equestrianism, croquet, and golf.

In the 1900 Olympic Games, Charlotte Cooper became the first female Olympic individual champion. She won the gold medal for the singles and mixed doubles competitions in tennis.

In the early twentieth century, women's suffrage (the fight for the right to vote, ratified by Congress in 1920) helped women gain more ground in the sports world, but the Great Depression (1929–1939) erased those advances. Women were needed at home. When women were asked to take jobs during World War II (1939–1945), women's equality gained a little more traction. As the war continued, women carried the early versions of equality from the workplace onto the sports field.

In 1943 the All-American Girls Softball League emerged, as a response to worries that Major League Baseball players would be serving in World War II. Chicago Cubs owner Philip Wrigley created the league with the goal of using baseball stadiums and engaging Major League Baseball audiences. The league lasted until 1954, through a few name changes (All-American Girls Baseball League, All-American Girls Professional Ball League, and American Girls Baseball League). Despite all the different monikers, no one ever got it quite right: the league was made of women softball players, not girls. Not many players were under eighteen, and the youngest players were fifteen—old enough to be considered young women. The players had to be good ballplayers but were also expected to be ladylike and attractive. They were issued beauty kits and were required to attend charm school in the evenings.

# TITLE IX

The official language of Title IX is as follows: "No person in the United States shall, on the basis of sex, be excluded from participation in, be denied the benefits of, or be subjected to discrimination under any education program or activity receiving Federal financial assistance."

The Civil Rights Act of 1964 and feminist activism helped push women's sports further in the 1960s. The Equal Rights Amendment, first proposed in the early 1900s by suffragette Alice Paul and reinvigorated in the late '60s and early '70s, also continued the conversation about women's sports.

After a few different tries to centralize an organization for women's sports, the Commission on Intercollegiate Athletics for Women emerged in 1967. By 1969 the commission had a schedule of national championships for gymnastics as well as track and field. National championships for swimming, badminton, and volleyball were organized for 1970, and basketball was added in 1972, after the formation of the Association for Intercollegiate Athletics for Women (AIAW) in 1971.

The Education Amendments of 1972 (sometimes called the Higher Education Amendments), which Title IX was part of, were used to update several other education laws from 1963 and 1965. Title IX was enacted by the Ninety-Second US Congress on June 23, 1972. Title IX states that no institution receiving federal funding can discriminate based on sex.

There is no language in Title IX specifically related to sports, but sports are part of the American school experience. Since schools benefit from federal funding, they were no longer allowed to offer a few sports for girls or women and many sports for boys or men.

# CONGRESSWOMAN PATSY MINK

Representative Patsy Takemoto Mink of Hawaii was the major author and sponsor of Title IX.

Mink was born and raised on the island of Maui before Hawaii was a state. She and her white husband, along with their daughter, faced discrimination for their interracial marriage. Mink was a lawyer and founded the Oahu Young Democrats in 1954. She was a representative to the territorial house of representatives before she ran for the state's one at-large seat in the House of Representatives, created after Hawaii became a state in 1959. She lost but ran again in 1964 when the state was given a second seat in the House of Representatives. Mink also served in the Hawaii state senate from 1962–1964.

Mink was the first Asian American and first woman of color in the House of Representatives. She served for twelve terms. She worked with Representatives Edith Starrett Green of Oregon and

Birch Bayh of Indiana to build support for Title IX's passage in 1972. In 1975 opponents tried to exempt school athletics from Title IX and succeeded by one vote—Mink was absent and unable to cast her vote because her daughter had been in a car accident. Mink's supporters defended her absence, and the vote was recalled and cast again. Title IX survived.

A school's Title IX compliance is evaluated by a comprehensive evaluation of both men's and women's sports (or boys' and girls' sports, in high school). Programs might spend different amounts of money on different sports for each group (men's football equipment might cost more than women's lacrosse equipment, for example), so money isn't one of the metrics. Compliance is having equal participation opportunities, equal scholarships for athletes, and equal access to equipment, travel resources, access to tutoring and coaching, training facilities, publicity, and recruitment, among other things.

Women's sports exploded after Title IX. Before 1972 fewer than five hundred thousand girls participated in high school programs. In 2018 the number had increased to three and a half million. In 1971 women college athletes numbered under fifty thousand. Currently, more than two hundred thousand women play college sports.

## RUTH BADER GINSBURG AND HER ROLE IN TITLE IX

Lawyer and Supreme Court justice Ruth Bader Ginsburg (1933–2020) was a force for women's equality. She spent much of her legal career before her appointment to the Supreme Court working on cases that included gender. In 1972 she took the case of Abbe Seldin of Teaneck, New Jersey, who wanted to play on her high school's varsity men's tennis team. Her school had no women's team, and she was a nationally ranked player. Ginsburg (then teaching at Rutgers Law School) and fellow American Civil Liberties Union volunteer Annamay Sheppard filed a case in New Jersey's District Court on her behalf. Halfway through the case, the New Jersey State Interscholastic Athletic Association changed its rules to allow female athletes to play particular sports, including tennis.

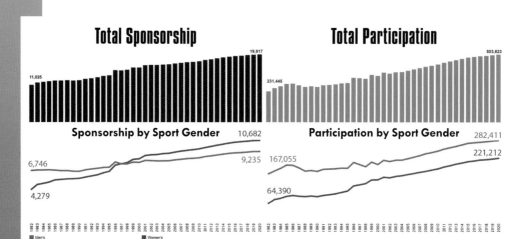

**Total Sponsorship**

11,025  19,917

Sponsorship by Sport Gender  10,682

6,746  9,235

4,279

**Total Participation**

231,445  503,623

Participation by Sport Gender  282,411

167,055  221,212

64,390

■ Men's    ■ Women's
Published: December 2020

**While men continue to participate in collegiate sports in higher numbers than women, the gap between the two has closed significantly in the past forty years.**

Did Title IX make everything equal and equitable for girls' and women's sports? No. The Women's Sports Foundation published a comprehensive report in early 2020, after surveying more than twenty-three hundred women's sports leaders (from coaches to journalists) in the US, and we have a long way to go. Access for women and girls in sports is still rising, but the gender gap remains and Title IX compliance is spotty at best. The foundation's report mentions a US Department of Education statistic that says 85 percent of schools in the NCAA, in all three divisions, offer more athletic opportunities to men (based on enrollment numbers).

## MYTHS ABOUT TITLE IX

People don't always know what Title IX does and doesn't support, so myths have grown up around Title IX since its inception. Title IX wasn't a popular law with men who stood to lose power or prestige. In 1975 John Fuzak, then president of the NCAA, remarked that using Title IX to improve athletics "borders on insanity that threatens to destroy many university athletic programs."

One of the biggest myths? Title IX means colleges have to cut men's athletic programs. Gender equity in sports opportunity is the key, and schools are free to increase or decrease both men's and women's programs to meet that equity. Another myth says schools must spend the same on men's and women's athletic programs. Schools must offer the same amount of money in scholarships to both male and female athletes, but otherwise, each set of programs will have its own equipment, coaching, and management expenses. But men's and women's programs must receive the same level of service, support, and quality equipment from their school. Another big myth? Title IX is controversial. Most of the public think that men and women should have the same sports opportunities. Within the sports world, Title IX opposition usually comes from people who've lost something in an equity fight related to Title IX.

Other myths? Title IX exists strictly to support women. It's there to support all genders. People also worry Title IX means all organizations or teams at a school have to include all genders. But single gender teams and clubs are absolutely acceptable.

A very significant Title IX myth that has grown up in the twenty-first century is that admitting trans women into women's sports

# TITLE IX, THE AIWA, AND THE NCAA

The NCAA has governed college sports since 1906, in response to repeated injuries and deaths in college football. Then there were no formal women's college sports. The NCAA works with everyone from college presidents to compliance officers to coaches and team personnel to be sure college sports (broken into three divisions by size of the college) are carefully administered. They "[prioritize] academics, well-being, and fairness so college athletes succeed on the field, in the classroom, and for life."

The NCAA didn't include women until the 1980s. Previously, women's collegiate sports had been governed by the Association for Intercollegiate Athletics for Women (AIAW). The AIAW was the result of several previous organizations and had over 280 schools as members in 1972 (it had almost 1,000 member schools at its peak). At that time, the NCAA wasn't interested in overseeing women's sports. The organizations had different policies and procedures for their student athletes.

After the passage of Title IX, the NCAA raised money to fight it. In 1974 the Tower Amendment was proposed, declaring football and other revenue-producing sports exempt from Title IX. The AIAW responded and fought the amendment, and it was defeated.

When schools discovered that women's sports could be profitable, the NCAA took note. It decided to offer some women's championships in the late 1970s, and merger conversations started. Members of the AIAW had many reservations about joining the two organizations.

In the March 1979 issue of *Athletic Business*, two governing women of the AIAW responded to the merger proposed by John Toner, the athletic director at the University of Connecticut. Kaye Hart and Carol Oglesby declared that the time was not right for the merger and that women would lose too much power over their programs. They were clear the merger would not be forced on

**AIAW was founded in 1971.**

women's programs. The women listed both general problems (not enough voting power for women and the idea that women are not a "special interest" group) and problems specific to athletics (staffing, financing, how to divide divisions, and committee and rules development) for their reasoning.

According to Hart and Oglesby, three standards would be met when the time had come for the merger: "First, women and men will be equally willing to make significant changes in their own organizations. For example, both the NCAA [and the AIAW] would modify their names and traditional geographic boundaries. Secondly, we will find that women and men have equal voice and vote in all matters that concern the new organization, from television contracts to international franchise disputes. Thirdly, women and men will have publicly acknowledged and actively pursued affirmative action steps to end age-old patterns of discrimination."

Their arguments eventually dissolved under the pressure of profits and what the NCAA could offer women's teams, especially related to championships, and many women's programs became members of the NCAA. The AIAW filed an antitrust lawsuit against the NCAA but lost. The AIAW was finished on June 30, 1983.

(something Title IX supports) will destroy women's sports. This argument is made by individuals who don't believe trans women are women (they believe trans women are men pretending to be women, and therefore are threatening to women). According to the Women's Liberation Front, a prominent transgender exclusionary feminist group, they will "defend sex-segregation of women's sports, bathrooms, and locker rooms" against trans women empowered by Title IX to join the sport that fits their gender identity.

Why did this myth begin? The interpretation of Title IX expanded. We'll talk more about this myth in chapter 3.

## HOW THE INTERPRETATION OF TITLE IX HAS CHANGED

It's not unusual for the interpretations of laws to expand as a society changes and grows, and Title IX is no exception. Many different challenges and amendments are part of its history. The 1974 Tower Amendment asked for revenue-producing sports at the college level to be exempted from Title IX, but it was defeated. In 1979 the US Supreme Court ruled that individuals can sue under Title IX. In 1984 the Supreme Court case *Grove City v. Bell* ruled that Title IX only applies to targeted funds within an institution, and sports are not included. The 1987 Civil Rights Restoration Act returned sports to Title IX protection.

More court rulings began to expand the protection afforded by Title IX. Beginning in 1992, students who suffered sexual harassment in schools were protected by Title IX. In 2005 teachers and coaches became protected by Title IX. If teachers and coaches suffered retaliation while protesting sex discrimination, they had a right to sue. Meanwhile, opponents were working to make Title IX enforcement less stringent. By 2005 colleges were allowed to email one survey to students to demonstrate that they were meeting women's sports needs.

Title IX's standards against sex discrimination have further been interpreted in the 2010s to include gender along with biological sex. LGBTQIA+ students have also sought protection in schools using Title IX. Challenges have been made to these broader, more inclusive uses for Title IX.

While President Barack Obama was in office, the Office for Civil Rights, the office within the Department of Education that administers Title IX, released its first "Dear Colleague" letter in April 2011. This document makes clear that sexual violence on college campuses (physical or verbal) can be prosecuted under Title IX, because sexual violence is discrimination based on sex. Colleges were required to follow this new interpretation of Title IX to receive federal funding.

This broadening of Title IX's interpretation was clarified with guidance in 2014—that guidance included language that mirrored the Equal Employment Opportunity Commission's 2012 language that solidified the Civil Rights Act's protection for transgender Americans. In the 2014 Title IX guidance, the OCR stated, "Title IX's sex discrimination prohibition extends to claims of discrimination based on gender identity or failure to conform to stereotypical notions of masculinity or femininity, and OCR accepts such complaints for investigation."

Protecting gender identity, gender expression, and sexual orientation with Title IX opened avenues for students (and parents, in K–12 settings) to hold schools accountable for bullying, harassment, and violence in new ways. Many educators welcomed it.

In May 2016, the US Departments of Justice and Education provided joint guidance about transgender students and Title IX protection. The information was specific and clear: "Both federal agencies treat a student's gender identity as the student's sex for purposes of enforcing Title IX." The guide was prompted by questions from schools about how to ensure the rights of transgender students, and schools received this very specific guidance: "A school may not

# THE SPORTS BRA

Sports bras didn't exist until after Title IX. In 1975 women were finally able to buy a bra called the Free Swing Tennis Bra, but it wasn't designed for sports with any type of impact such as running or jogging. The straps were still thin and would often fall off the shoulders. In 1977 a woman named Lisa Lindahl got a call from her sister, asking what bra she used to run in. Lindahl asked her friend, Polly Smith, a costume designer, to help make a prototype bra that would be comfortable for women's exercise. Smith would design something, and Lindahl would test it.

But the modern sports bra didn't take shape until after Lindahl's then husband suggested they should model it after a jockstrap. Lindahl and Smith went to work, made a prototype, found an investor, and the jockbra was born. The name was later changed to the jogbra.

Lindahl wanted the bra to be modest enough that women could wear it without a shirt (her regular running partner was a man, and she was envious of his ability to remove his shirt while they ran). If you look at current women's beach volleyball uniforms—or the famous photo of Brandi Chastain celebrating her winning penalty kick in the 1999 FIFA Women's World Cup that secured the World Cup for the US women—you know that Lindahl's invention has been worn alone as well as under countless women's sports uniforms and workout shirts.

Brandi Chastain's celebration at the 1999 FIFA Women's World Cup is an iconic moment in sports history—thanks in part to the development of the jockbra twenty years earlier.

Tennis bras that came out in the mid-1970s did not fill the need for a supportive bra to wear when playing sports, and advertisements for them didn't market them for use when running or jogging.

Lindahl chose to market her product to sporting goods stores rather than department stores. She wanted the bra to be available where serious sporting goods were sold—the bra was intended to be a serious piece of athletic equipment.

Lindahl was watching when Chastain scored that penalty kick, and she saw Chastain strip off her shirt, just as male soccer players do when they win big games. It was a full-circle moment for the inventor of the sports bra. Lindahl says, "And there it was, right on—not just national TV, it was international—there are people all over the globe watching that. When [Chastain is] asked about that moment she talks about it being a long journey, You know, a long accumulation of effort and work, and that's what my life has been—it's like the two of us coming from two very different places, it all sort of came together in that moment of women's power and glory and truthfulness. And that was a moment of true beauty. Oh, by the way, thank you Brandi."

require transgender students to have a medical diagnosis, undergo any medical treatment, or produce a birth certificate or other identification document before treating them consistent with their gender identity." This information was a groundbreaking use of Title IX protections.

Those specific transgender policies lasted less than a year. President Donald Trump took office in January 2017, and Secretary of Education Betsy DeVos rescinded these policies in February 2017. Critics of the policies enacted under Obama were happy to see them end. With their removal, protections for transgender students were particularly eroded. In 2019 three high school track athletes in Connecticut filed a complaint with their school district under Title IX to prevent them from having to compete against transgender girls. They claimed transgender girls have an unfair advantage in athletics because they have physiologically male body characteristics. In 2020 the district was asked to change its policy, even though Connecticut state law prohibits discrimination on the basis of gender identity. The state's attorney general opposed the ruling for the students, as did the Connecticut Interscholastic Athletic Conference.

On January 8, 2021, DeVos wrote one last policy memorandum about a Supreme Court case, *Bostock v. Clayton County*, decided in 2020. The case decided that Title VII of the Civil Rights Act (signed into law by President Lyndon Johnson in 1964) protects employees from being fired because of their sexual orientation or their gender identity. DeVos's memorandum

During her time as secretary of education, DeVos rolled back protections for transgender students as well as sexual assault survivors on college and university campuses.

# THE COMPLEXITIES OF SEX AND GENDER

Sex and gender are not the same thing. Both are broader and more complex than the binaries we traditionally give them (sex: male and female, gender: man and woman). Sex generally refers to biology and the genetic factors of our bodies—such as chromosomes, genitalia, and hormones. Not everyone falls into the binary categories we sort them into. Some individuals are born with different chromosomal makeups (XXY or XYY) or mixed genitalia. It used to be that parents of children with mixed genitalia would choose the gender of that child and surgery would be performed, but now surgery usually waits until children express their gender.

Despite not knowing exactly who we are, when we're born we're assigned a gender (male or female) by doctors, based on our genitalia. Sometimes that assignment fits our gender identity as it develops, and we're cisgender—someone assigned female at birth who identifies as a woman, for example. Sometimes it doesn't, and we're transgender—for example, someone assigned male at birth who expresses her gender as a woman. Some transgender individuals change their bodies to match their gender identity, and some don't.

Gender is an identification of who we are, and our gender identification comes from our brain. Our gender tells us our pronouns (he, she, or they). It happens partially in response to cultural roles and environment, but it's not given to us—we know it in our minds. Sometimes our gender identification and expression (such as clothes, hairstyles, names, and jobs) fit the cultural binaries of men and women, and sometimes they don't.

All of these differences in sex and gender are natural human variation. The sports world, however, has been highly binary, for many different reasons. Hopefully, time will allow for larger expressions of gender and sex differences in sports.

clarified that *Bostock v. Clayton County* does not apply to Title IX, and that the traditional reading of sex as binary and strictly biological would continue to be Trump's education policy.

When Biden took office twelve days later, on January 20, he reversed the Title IX positions created by Trump and DeVos in early 2017. On his first day in office, he signed an executive order referencing *Bostock v. Clayton County*, Title VII, and Title IX. Though it doesn't explicitly address sports, the executive order guides all federal agencies to include sexual orientation and gender identity when enforcing federal laws barring sex discrimination, as *Bostock* clarified. These federal agencies relate to housing, employment, education, health care, and banking, among other institutions. The only reference to sports was this: "Children should be allowed to learn without worrying about whether they will be denied access to the restroom, the locker room, or school sports." Immediately, supporters of Trump's policies claimed that women's sports would be destroyed by the biological advantage transgender girls and women would have while playing on girls' and women's sports teams.

In February 2021, White House press secretary Jen Psaki affirmed the Biden administration's position on trans girls and women in sports. When a reporter asked her to clarify the administration's position about trans and cis girls competing against each other in sports, Psaki reiterated that the president understood the impact of his executive order, and that trans rights are human rights.

As the twenty-first century progresses, there will be new interpretations and memorandums to Title IX. Hopefully, those changes will move toward even more inclusion and protection for all athletes. The enforcement of Title IX will continue to tear down barriers erected by systems that affect young athletes. But Title IX can't eliminate sexism and its influences. People have to do that.

Another barrier Title IX can't fight is the struggles for equity and equality that women's amateur and professional athletes face.

Why doesn't our culture support these athletes once they leave school? Those athletes are relying on us to support their athletic success. Title IX can't remedy how women's amateur and professional sports teams, players, and coaches are regarded by the public.

**White House press secretary Jen Psaki at the media briefing on February 9, 2021**

Sexism created the need for Title IX, and sexism continues to harm girls' and women's sports. We still need to fight sexism so Title IX can work as it's designed to, and so professional women's sports have more equitable opportunities to show the world their excellence.

# CHAPTER 3

# Before and after Title IX

Title IX complaints and court cases are continually being argued and settled in the United States. These cases are filed on behalf of students ranging from elementary school to college, and the cases cover many angles of Title IX support, from sexual harassment to equity for trans students to inequitable support of men's and women's sports teams. Because of the ever-changing nature of these cases, you will need to do an internet search to find the relevant ones.

Title IX has helped more girls and women get into amateur and professional sports. But Title IX is only a Band-Aid. Systemic gender inequity—sexism—is the ultimate barrier to equity and equality, whether it's before, after, or beyond Title IX.

## KATHRINE SWITZER AND THE BOSTON MARATHON

Several years before Title IX, nineteen-year-old Kathrine Switzer attended Syracuse University as a journalism major. It was 1966, and she wanted to run competitively, but there was no women's running team. She began training with the men's cross-country team. In mid-December, she was running with her coach and mentor, Arnie Briggs, a veteran of many Boston Marathons, and she declared she wanted to run the race. Briggs first argued that women were too fragile to run the Boston Marathon. Then he said she had to prove it to him.

So she did. She and Briggs were ready for the race on Wednesday, April 19, 1967. Switzer's boyfriend, also an athlete (football and hammer throw), signed up to run with them. He figured if a girl could run a marathon, he could too. When she entered, she signed her name K. V. Switzer, as she always did. There was no information about gender on the entry form or in the rule book. Switzer was very nervous the night before the race, but her dad reassured her she had trained and was ready.

During the warm-up, most fellow runners seemed welcoming of Switzer and she felt comfortable. Her numbers were pinned to the front and back of her sweatshirt (it was a cold and wet day), and she was ready to go. Her boyfriend, however, wanted her to remove her lipstick, in case someone objected to her running the race. She refused. She didn't want attention, but she also wasn't shy about being present. One man actually had his wife take a picture of Switzer and him together before the race began. As the race began, her running companions gained extra attention because of her presence, and they loved it.

Around mile 4 (6 k), the press truck came through the runners and was surprised to see a woman in their midst. They took several photos. Then Switzer saw a man in an overcoat standing in the middle of the street, shaking his finger at her. She noticed a ribbon on his chest that marked him as an official of the Boston Athletic Association, the organization that ran the Boston Marathon. After she saw him, she heard footsteps behind her, and a man she didn't know—who knew her coach, Briggs, and spoke to him—tried to rip the number off her front.

After Switzer ran in the 1967 Boston Marathon, the Amateur Athletic Union (AAU) banned women from competing in races with men. It would be five more years before the Boston Marathon ran an official women's race.

While she worked to get away, he ripped the number off her back.

Here is an excerpt from Switzer's 2007 memoir *Marathon Woman: Running the Race to Revolutionize Women's Sports.* An updated memoir was released in 2017, to coincide with the fiftieth anniversary of Switzer's harrowing race.

> The air was filled only with the clicking whirr of motor-drive cameras, scuffling sounds, and faintly, one cameraman screeching something I couldn't understand. The bottom was dropping out of my stomach; I had never felt such embarrassment and fear. I'd never been manhandled, never even spanked as a child, and the physical power and swiftness of the attack stunned me. I felt unable to flee, like I was rooted there, and indeed I was, because the man, this Jock guy [who knew her coach], had me by the shirt. Then a flash of orange flew past and hit Jock with a cross-body block.

It was Big Tom [her boyfriend], in the orange Syracuse sweatshirt. There was a thud—whoomph!—and Jock was airborne. He landed on the roadside like a pile of wrinkled clothes. Now I felt terror. We've killed this guy Jock. It's my fault, even though hothead Tom did it. My God, we're all going to jail. Then I saw Arnie's face—it was full of fear, too; his eyes were goggled and he shouted, "Run like hell!" All the adrenaline kicked in and down the street we ran, flying past the press truck, running like kids out of a haunted house.

The press truck eventually caught up to them and started asking Switzer questions. Switzer said, "I made it clear that I was not trying to 'prove' anything except that I wanted to run, I'd trained seriously for the distance, and I was not going to drop out. They wrote down what they wanted to write down. Clearly, they didn't believe me, as they stayed alongside. They thought it was a prank and didn't want to miss the moment when I'd give up. This made me even more resolved. In fact, it infuriated me."

Switzer and Briggs swore to finish the race, even though they feared they'd be arrested at the end of it. Switzer's boyfriend Tom appeared to drop out because he was convinced he'd never make the Olympic team, since he'd hit a race official—and it was all Switzer's fault. She was ashamed by his accusation, but she didn't quit. Her mind was so busy sorting out the attack and Tom's accusation that she didn't even notice she'd run over the course's notorious Heartbreak Hill.

At the race's end, she talked to reporters. Then she, Briggs, and their Syracuse cross-country team running companion had a steak dinner with Briggs's friends in Boston and headed back to Syracuse, a five-hour drive from Boston. When they pulled over to get coffee and gas at one in the morning, Switzer saw one of the previous evening's newspapers. Photos of her were all over it. Even if her male companions didn't recognize the weight of what she'd just accomplished, she felt it. She knew the sports world had just changed.

After the marathon, Switzer became a champion for women and worked to create change for women athletes as well as women as a whole. She's run thirty-nine marathons and has worked in public relations and marketing for sports and large corporate brands. She's also a public speaker, broadcaster, and writer. She says her run is still the most important hour of her day. In 2017 she ran the Boston Marathon again to celebrate the fiftieth anniversary of her first time on the course.

## WHY DO WE HAVE MEN'S AND WOMEN'S DEODORANT?

Men and women athletes sweat—a lot. But men's deodorant is cheaper. Why?

It's called the pink tax.

The "pink tax" is defined as the extra money women pay for particular products or services. Its more formal title is "price discrimination," or gendered pricing. It means women will pay more for pink razors, but the razors will be the same as the blue ones packaged for men. Women pay more than men almost half the time for essentially the same products. The pink tax applies to clothes, girls' toys, personal care products, and dry cleaning, and amounts to about $1,300 per year.

Some women athletes might choose or want to pay more for particular smells or packages that women's products have, but some might care more about saving money. As one women's soccer player and college crew (rowing) member said, "An 'underarm' is still an armpit. We all use men's deodorant. It's cheaper."

During the COVID-19 pandemic, beginning in 2020, colleges and universities lost money, similar to many other institutions and businesses in America. To offset the revenue losses from fewer students and fewer moneymaking opportunities, including sports, colleges and universities began cutting budgets. For many schools, these cuts involved entire sports teams. But athletes and watchdog groups outside of schools question whether these women's team cuts are Title IX violations.

ESPN.com reported that 352 NCAA sports programs have been cut between March and October 2020—and the majority of them are Olympic sports, thus changing the number of programs Olympic hopefuls can train with. Of the closed programs, 132 were women's sports. Women still have fewer opportunities to compete in sports at the college level, so cutting any programs is potentially a Title IX violation. Schools are regularly in Title IX violation but aren't often sanctioned for it.

To be Title IX compliant, a school must meet one of the three "prongs," or tests, of Title IX. If a school can demonstrate it meets the criteria of the prong, a Title IX case won't proceed. One Title IX test is proportionality. If a school's student body is 45 percent men and 55 percent women, their sports programs should also follow that same proportion—45 percent of the teams are men's teams, and 55 percent are women's teams. Another Title IX test is expansion. If a school has previously had fewer opportunities for women athletes but is working on creating more, the school may be seen as Title IX compliant.

The third Title IX test relates to accommodating the sports interests of the student body. If a school can demonstrate that the women on campus are satisfied with the sports opportunities provided (whether they're formal teams or extracurricular teams), the school may be compliant with Title IX. Schools have to make active efforts to survey the student body, as well as respond positively to requests for more sports teams for women.

In the fall of 2020, the University of Iowa decided to cut its women's swimming and diving teams due to pandemic money issues but reversed its decision in February 2021, following a court injunction ordering it to reinstate the teams. Because the university has proportionately fewer opportunities for women to compete in sports, the cuts are a Title IX violation. But, because of the cuts, the university is still facing a class-action lawsuit (involving current and future students, not just the people who originated the lawsuit). According to women's swim team captain Sage Ohlensehlen, "I understand that our teams don't make as much money as football and basketball . . . but we trained just as hard and we have just as much love for our sport. We deserve to play just as much as any other athlete. . . . I am sick and tired of being treated like I am second rate. I plan on standing up for what is right and fighting for equality."

Other schools that have cut women's teams include Stanford University, Clemson University, George Washington University, and San Diego State University. The University of Connecticut and Dartmouth College are facing Title IX suits due to their cuts, and Title IX lawsuits (or threats of them) have been settled at Brown University, William and Mary, and East Carolina State University.

At the University of Minnesota, the cuts were made to men's teams: gymnastics, indoor and outdoor track and field, and tennis. The statement from the university president and athletic director said the cuts would align their participation numbers and their undergraduate percentages: "By having our program offerings mirror our changing student population, the University will be ensuring that we are providing full, effective, and equitable participation opportunities for our female and male student-athletes."

Former Minnesota athlete and public policy professor Elizabeth Sharrow sees the statement differently. Sharrow argues that the statement pits men's teams against women's, a mistake that stirs up opposition to Title IX as well as obscures other ways to handle a budget shortfall. If the University of Minnesota reduced its football roster and cut football team spending (its most profitable program, which was unable to generate much revenue during the pandemic), the men's sports teams could be saved. Sharrow says, "The incomplete picture Gopher Athletics paints of its commitment to Title IX glosses over inequitable practices, ignores alternative solutions which could better address the financial strain, and fundamentally undermines the pursuit of gender equity more broadly."

Donna Lopiano, a Title IX expert, and president of Sports Management Resources, agrees. She argues that athletic revenue can be rearranged to protect women's programs: "Everyone knows . . . [schools] are losing money. It's intuitive . . . to cut back, but any athletic director worth their oats knows that they don't have to cut any sports in order to keep their athletic program intact. They just have to reduce expenses." Revenue also factors into the cuts. Few sports teams at a college will produce revenue, but cuts happen often to the women's nonrevenue teams.

Nancy Hogshead-Makar is an Olympic athlete, lawyer, and founder of Champion Women, an advocacy organization for women athletes. She sees these cuts as highly damaging, on several levels: "People talk about 'Title IX compliance.' We have got to move away from that language because it doesn't represent the harm that is being done to girls and women. Instead call it what it is; athletic departments are engaged in institutionalized, intentional sex discrimination. . . . The truth is, people are really getting hurt: the 183,000 girls and women who don't have college teams waiting for them or who don't get a college scholarship because of discrimination. Women are a billion dollars behind men in college scholarships. A billion! Because they are women. No other reason."

The billion-dollar figure comes from the analysis of public data from the US Department of Education's Equity in Athletics report, completed by Champion Women. They discovered that 90 percent of the 2,072 colleges and universities with data in the report actively discriminate against women who play intercollegiate sports. When Champion Women figured equity using playing opportunities, recruiting money, and scholarships, less than 1 percent of the schools passed the test.

Starting in 2015, Champion Women began sharing this data with the schools that sent data to the report. Champion Women wanted these schools to understand how underrepresented women still were in their sports programs. The organization saw no change, no matter whether they sent letters to presidents, faculty, athletic directors, or anyone else. In the summer of 2020, Champion Women changed tactics. They sent letters directly to athletic conferences about these equity gaps, and they also began gathering women athletes together on Zoom calls to talk about the inequalities. These Zoom calls seem to have made a difference—the recent Title IX suits related to pandemic cuts have all come from students.

Hogshead-Makar says, "The core of Title IX always comes back to a well-settled principle: that men and women are entitled to equal educational opportunities."

## THE US WOMEN'S NATIONAL SOCCER TEAM AND THEIR FIGHT FOR EQUITY

Some college athletes work hard to turn pro, and some also go on to play on our national teams. The US women's national soccer team has won four world championships and four Olympic gold medals. They're one of the most decorated teams in American history, and the most decorated women's soccer team in the world. The team was launched after Title IX prompted many colleges to create women's soccer programs. International women's soccer was also gaining popularity around then.

The US women's national soccer team got its start when a team was formed to play in an Italian tournament in 1985 (comprised of women's college players). The team then hired a full-time manager in 1986. The team won the first Women's World Cup, sponsored by FIFA, in 1991. Their victory in July 1999's World Cup—with an audience of more than ninety thousand filling the Rose Bowl in Pasadena, California—inspired many American girls to take up soccer. They were honored with a ticker-tape parade in New York City for their 2015 Women's World Cup victory, the first time such a parade has been hosted for women's sports, and were also honored by Obama at the White House.

In March 2016, five well-known players—Carli Lloyd, Megan Rapinoe, Hope Solo, Alex Morgan, and Becky Sauerbrunn—filed a wage discrimination complaint with the Equal Employment Opportunity Commission, against the U.S. Soccer Federation. The complaint claimed that the achievements and popularity of the team had not resulted in them earning equal to or more than their men's national team counterparts. Even though the women had earned more than $20 million more in revenue during 2015 than the men's team had, they were paid almost four times less than male players. Other benefits were also less—men were allowed seventy-five dollars a day to cover food during international travel, while women received sixty dollars. No decision was ever filed about the complaint.

The team continued to press for equity by filing a gender discrimination lawsuit against the U.S. Soccer Federation on March 8, 2019. This lawsuit ended their wage discrimination complaint filed three years earlier. Twenty-eight team members were named as plaintiffs, and the team alleged "institutionalized gender discrimination." The suit sought to establish equality with the men's team in pay and treatment, and the suit also asked for back pay and other damages. The team did gain changes and benefits through collective bargaining negotiations for their 2017–2021 work contract.

As the suit was filed and directly afterward, the US women's national team continued their popularity as they worked toward winning the 2019 World Cup. In July 2019, as the team worked through the semifinals stage of the tournament, the home jersey for the US women's national team became the best-selling soccer jersey sold in one season, for men's or women's teams. It was the top-selling soccer jersey ever sold on Nike.com in one season, and sales were 500 percent greater than they were in 2015 at the semifinals mark of the previous World Cup.

Immediately after the championship game on July 7, 2019, the World Cup crowd in Lyon, France, took the side of the USWNT. They chanted "equal pay" as the team celebrated their victory on the field. According to spectators and reporters, the chant was "deafening."

After the World Cup, the sides went back and forth several times, about several different angles of the case. In late July 2019, the USSF released figures that claimed the women had been paid more in salaries and bonuses than the men had been, from 2010 to 2018. The USWNT disagreed. In November 2019, the lawsuit was made a class-action suit. USSF president Carlos Cordeiro resigned in March 2020 over language that was seen as demeaning to women's soccer and women's sports as a whole. The USSF had filed court documents claiming the work by the women's team wasn't of equal effort, skill, or responsibility to the men's team. It wasn't the first time the USSF had made such claims.

The COVID-19 pandemic rearranged some trial dates in 2020, but the trial continued. In May 2020 a judge ruled in favor of the U.S. Soccer Federation, saying the differences between collective bargaining agreements for the men's and women's teams accounted for the salary and bonus differences, but other benefits in the women's contract evens out the total amount players receive. The women's team vowed to keep fighting for equal pay. In December 2020 the USWNT and USSF resolved their dispute about equal working conditions. The USSF agreed to create policies to ensure equity with the men's team related to staff, places to play, and travel, including hotels. The team will continue to appeal the May 2020 pay decision. The president of USSF, Cindy Parlow Cone, also a former USWNT member, said that making up the back

**A fan holds up a sign in support of the USWNT's fight for equal pay at the 2020 SheBelieves Cup.**

pay for the team would most likely bankrupt the organization. In July 2021, the USWNT filed an opening brief in their appeal with the Ninth Circuit Court of Appeals. The US men's national team filed an amicus brief, a legal document created to support a court case by people not involved in the case, with the court later in the month, indicating their support of the women's team and their fight.

In the February 2021 issue of *GQ*, Megan Rapinoe shared her frustration with having to convince people she deserves to be paid what she's worth: "I'm ******* sick of convincing people that I'm great at my job . . . *clearly* I'm great at my job! We did everything on the field. We pretty much did everything off the field. We're good role models, you know? We are profitable. For them to consistently dig their heels in on an issue [where] it's very clear where the world is going is a colossal waste of time [for them]."

In September 2021, the U.S. Soccer Federation announced they would offer the same players' union contracts to both the men's and women's teams. Though pay differences still remain related to prize money, the contract decision shifts both teams to an equal pay structure, if the unions choose to accept the contract.

# WHAT WOMEN ATHLETES WEAR

Sexism affects sports in many different ways. An example is whether women's athletic clothing and sports uniforms are designed to be sexy. Athletic clothes and sports uniforms are created in specific ways to assist an athlete's performance—often to promote easy movement and provide less restriction. But sports observers question whether women athletes need to be attractive to decision makers (usually straight men) to get those men to take them seriously, and whether uniform design is part of that attraction.

After the 2016 Olympics, gender-nonconforming model Rain Dove completed a photo series wearing athletic clothes from various Olympic sports. Dove posed in both typical men's and women's clothing for particular sports throughout the series, to compare what each gender wears to compete. Dove viewed the women's clothes as "sexploitation." According to Dove, "I think some [uniforms] are designed for the actual sport and some are designed specifically to sell the sport. . . . People want to watch women [athletes] not because of their skills but because of their bodies"

In an editorial for their Illinois high school newspaper, the *Evanstonian*, writers Ben Baker-Katz and Hailey Fine contemplated similar questions about women's sports uniforms, especially skirts for girls' lacrosse, field hockey, and tennis uniforms as well as tight spandex shorts for girls' volleyball. The writers say they've heard from guys who love watching volleyball, strictly for the uniforms. The pair argues, "Women were thought of as masculine if they played a sport, so in an attempt to hide this 'masculinity' they wore slim fitting clothes and skirts. Some may argue that skirts are more comfortable and easier to play in, but aren't shorts just as comfortable? Shorts won't ride up when you sprint, or become too revealing when you bend over. If the two options are equally as comfortable, why is it that girls are still wearing a uniform that was born from the idea of keeping women out of men's sports?"

Gymnasts and fans alike responded positively to the German team's unitards, and many emphasized the importance of making sure athletes feel comfortable and confident in competition wear.

Baker-Katz and Fine know these problems aren't just in their high school but exist in larger sports culture. They conclude, "It's time for girls to have the freedom to wear uniforms that won't sexualize their bodies and make them seem as though they are any less than the guys that play the same sport as them."

The 2020 Tokyo Olympics, held in July and August 2021, saw one women's team fighting back against sexist uniforms. The German gymnastics team chose to wear unitards rather than leotards, covering themselves from shoulders to ankle. The team also wore them in the European championships, in April 2021. Both the gymnasts and the coaches agreed that the move was about confidence and comfort, as well as fighting against the sexualization of gymnastics. According to gymnast Sarah Voss, "In the sport of gymnastics it gets harder and harder [to feel good in your skin] as you grow out of your child's body. As a little girl I didn't see the tight gym outfits as such a big deal. But when puberty began, when my period came, I began feeling increasingly uncomfortable."

Right before the Olympics, the Norwegian beach handball team exchanged the required bikini bottoms of their uniforms for shorts during the European Beach Handball Championship. As a result, the team was fined £1,295 (about $1,800). American pop singer Pink offered to pay their fine, in thanks for taking a stand against sexism.

## THE FIGHTS AROUND TRANSGENDER WOMEN ATHLETES

Individuals both inside and outside the sports world have many different opinions about whether transgender women and girls should be allowed to compete with cisgender women. These discussions are often heated and complicated by biases and incorrect information.

Sometimes individuals want to debate whether transgender women are actually women, but that debate has been answered by science. Although we're assigned a sex at birth, researchers and scientists know that anatomy isn't everything. Dr. Joshua Safer, a professor of endocrinology at Mount Sinai Health System, says, "The idea that a person's sex is determined by their anatomy at birth is not true, and we've known that it's not true for decades." Scientists aren't entirely sure what creates our gender identity, but Safer says, "We know that there is a significant, durable biological underpinning to gender identity . . . what we don't know are all of the biological factors at play that explain gender identity." Researchers know gender identity comes from our brains, and it's not based on how our bodies present themselves. No one is sure why it happens sometimes—a person's brain says one thing, while their body says another. Safer is clear that being transgender is neither a fad nor a whim.

While people can choose how they express their gender (what they wear, their name, and whether they show or hide their transgender self), they can't choose their gender. Simón(e) D. Sun says in a blog post for *Scientific American*, "Transgender humans represent the complexity and diversity that are fundamental features of life, evolution and nature itself."

Why are people so concerned about trans women athletes? Because trans women are assigned male at birth. Opponents of transgender inclusion in sports claim trans women have an advantage over cisgender women, due to their testosterone levels and the physical developments it causes. Testosterone is the human hormone that helps males be generally bigger and stronger than females. Adding testosterone to your body is illegal in sports and is considered "doping," because it can give you a competitive advantage. However, most athletic policies create parameters for testosterone levels in trans women, though this limitation also has objections. There's no set scientific limit for what constitutes an "advantage" for women's testosterone levels. Cisgender women also have testosterone, and regulating testosterone levels for transgender *or* cisgender women amounts to policing women's bodies.

In 2014 researchers in Britain and Ireland profiled 693 elite cisgender athletes and measured their testosterone levels. About 17 percent of men had lower testosterone levels than the lowest "normal range" numbers for men, and around 14 percent of women had higher testosterone levels than the highest "normal range" numbers for women. Is regulating hormone levels akin to regulating other natural features of an athlete, such as longer arms for a swimmer or extra height for a basketball player? Sheree Bekker argues that this policing

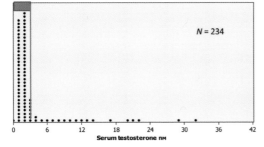

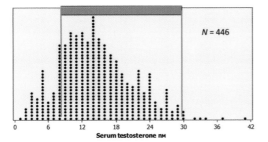

**While most of the athletes measured within the "normal range" of testosterone levels for their gender (as indicated by the gray bar), 16.5 percent of men fell below their lower bound, while 13.7 percent of women fell above their upper bound.**

**Masilingi (*left*) and Mboma celebrate Mboma's silver in the women's 200-meter dash at the 2020 Tokyo Olympics.**

of women's bodies is framed as fairness to cisgender women and doesn't protect all women's bodies, including transgender and intersex women. Bekker says that testosterone levels will vary from day to day for most humans, related to their age, health, stress levels, and other factors.

Hormonal gatekeeping affects both transgender and cisgender women. In early July 2021, before they were to compete in the postponed 2020 Tokyo Olympics, Namibian cisgender runners Christine Mboma and Beatrice Masilingi were banned from competing in the 400-meter race because of their naturally high testosterone levels. The women were shocked by the ruling—they had never been tested for testosterone levels before. Both women are eighteen, and neither want to take medication to reduce their testosterone, because it would alter their natural hormonal composition. Masilingi said, "I wouldn't want to involve any other things because this is the way my body functions in its normal way. And if I try something else, I might get caught somewhere else, and something might go wrong with my body" The testosterone rule, created by track and field's governing organization World Athletics, applies to races between 400 meters and a mile (1,609 m).

Trans women athletes can suffer injustice even after they compete.

Powerlifter Mary Gregory had lifting records taken away from her when she outed herself as a transgender woman. After a tournament in April 2019, she posted a photo of herself with her new trophy on Instagram, talking proudly about her new age and weight class records and thanking the tournament staff for treating her like any other woman. After the competition, and after the organization made Gregory provide a urine sample to test for drugs—a routine procedure for winners, but a test they had to watch, after they claimed the first test was botched—the 100% Raw Powerlifting Federation rescinded her records and banned her from competition. Gregory had checked the regulations for the tournament before she entered but saw no prohibition for trans women. She had been on hormone replacement therapy for a year prior to the tournament. Gregory says, she had to "work my ass off" for her wins. Before her tournament training, she noticed significant losses in the amount she could lift, thanks to her testosterone suppressant. But those losses prompted her to train even harder. Gregory believes testosterone is only part of the equation when it comes to athletic performance: "There are so many other factors that determine how much you lift: biomechanics, better leverages,

Following the 100% Raw Powerlifting Federation's decision to pull her records, Gregory decided to become a referee with the American Powerlifting Federation.

# CASTER SEMENYA AND HER GENDER

South African middle-distance runner Caster Semenya doesn't struggle with her gender, but the sports world does. She was assigned female at birth, was raised as a girl, and identifies as a cisgender woman. However, in 2009, after her gold medal in the 800-meter race at the World Championships, officials from the International Association of Athletics Federations (IAAF) gave her genetic tests, claiming they were doping tests. Officials were suspicious about her speed and her rapid improvements. Though the results of those tests have never been disclosed, some information was leaked. It is assumed Semenya has a difference of sex development (DSD), an intersex condition, that results in her having higher levels of testosterone than most women.

The IAAF announced in July 2010 that Semenya could again compete in women's races, but she had to take medication to lower her testosterone. New rules for women with hyperandrogenism (high testosterone) were created, and a testosterone level was set. Semenya won silver medals for her 800-meter performances in both the 2011 Worlds and the 2012 Olympics, but both medals were moved to golds when the winner was found guilty of doping.

In 2014 another runner, Dutee Chand of India, appealed to the Court of Arbitration for Sport (CAS, an independent sports authority based in Switzerland) to lift her lifelong ban from the sport, due to high testosterone levels. She was cleared to compete in July 2015 by the sports authority as it suspended the IAAF's testosterone rules for two years. So, Semenya was able to compete, and she won the 800-meter gold medal in the 2016 Olympics. But the IAAF challenged the sports authority's ruling and then created new rulings about testosterone levels in 2018. The new regulations happened after the IAAF commissioned research regarding high testosterone levels and competitive advantages for women. The new level was set well above the levels most women would have, to account for variation. If a hyperandrogenic woman, such as Semenya or Chand, didn't want to alter their testosterone levels, they could move into shorter- or longer-distance races, participate in non-international races, or compete against men. The ruling affects middle-distance races, the ones Semenya was regularly winning.

**Semenya (*center*) holds up her gold medal after winning the women's 800-meter run at the 2016 Rio Olympics.**

In 2019 Semenya challenged the new IAAF rule in the Court of Arbitration for Sport, but the CAS ruled against her in May. The ruling, CAS said, was to protect the integrity of women's sports.

In September 2020 Semenya lost her appeal of the ruling. Human Rights Watch, an international group that tracks rights abuses, says that the ruling is detrimental to all women athletes, in part due to the surveillance it will require. They say, "Identifying which athletes are impacted by the regulations will be done through subjecting all women athletes' bodies to public scrutiny and requiring those that seem 'suspect' to undergo a medical examination. Men athletes are subject to no such surveillance or medical tests."

After the decision, Semenya said she will "continue to fight for the human rights of female athletes, both on the track and off, until we can all run free the way we were born."

Semenya filed another appeal in February 2021 against the CAS ruling with the European Court of Human Rights. Though she ran in the 5,000-meter qualifying race, which is not restricted by World Athletics' testosterone rule, she did not qualify for the July 2021 Tokyo Olympics.

Three other women born with a DSD condition were also stopped from running shorter races at the 2020 Tokyo Olympics due to their elevated testosterone levels: Burundi's Francine Niyonsaba, Kenya's Margaret Wambui, and Niger's Aminatou Seyni.

In October 2021, publisher W. W. Norton acquired Semenya's memoir, *Silence All the Noise.*

joints, length of bones—where do we stop and draw the line?—socioeconomics and access to nutrition and coaching and gyms."

Gregory believes that the 100% Raw Powerlifting Federation took their actions because they received so much criticism for allowing a trans woman to compete. The organization claimed they'd create a category for transgender lifters, but Gregory sees that plan as discriminatory. Her sense of accomplishment doesn't come from the records but from the sport itself. She says, "I can't quit. . . . Lifting is too important to me."

Many national and international organizations have policies about transgender women and non-binary competitors. Transathlete.com is run by trans man Chris Mosier, an athlete who competed on the US sprint duathlon national team for the World Championships in 2015 (a duathlon is similar to a triathlon, but the three legs are running, cycling, and running). The website has separate pages to catalog policies for K–12 sports, college sports, various sports organizations, and professional sports, pointing out the policies that are harmful or exclusionary. Only one professional women's sport—the National Women's Hockey League—has a policy about transgender women. They welcome trans women and non-binary competitors, and no athlete has to have gender confirmation surgery or a legal name change to play. The athlete must have testosterone levels within the typical range for women athletes.

The NCAA, which oversees Division I, II, and III sports at many colleges, has had its transgender student-athlete policy since 2011. Trans student-athletes don't need gender-confirming surgery or legal name changes to compete, but gender-affirming hormones make a difference. Trans women must have one year of hormone treatment to compete on a women's team (taking estrogen, or suppressing testosterone). Trans men (men assigned female at birth) must stop competing on women's teams when they start taking testosterone. Many colleges that aren't a part of the NCAA also have policies for trans athletes, as does the National Intramural-Recreational Sports Association. Some small sports conferences also have transgender athletic policies.

For younger transgender athletes, there are no set policies, and the application of national Title IX guidelines varies widely. Misinformation and discrimination are rampant in the K–12 school system about trans children. By summer 2021, roughly three-quarters of US states had bills introduced in their legislatures that would ban transgender girls from sports. In March 2020 Governor Brad Little of Idaho signed two anti-transgender bills into law. One prevents transgender girls from competing in sports, from kindergarten to the college level. Experts assume the laws won't hold up in court. In February 2021 Georgia legislators introduced a bill to allow physicians to examine the genitals of transgender girls who want to play sports. Gender would be defined as "a person's biological sex at birth," and transgender girls who wish to play would have to request a hearing. There, they would be examined by doctors. Like the Idaho law, experts agree this bill would be found illegal.

The Minnesota House anti-transgender bill introduced in February 2021 had the terrible distinction of being the first anti-transgender law in the country to criminalize a transgender girl's participation in sports. If a transgender girl or a cisgender boy attempted to play on a girls' team or use the girls' bathroom or locker room, they could be charged with a misdemeanor. But neither the Minnesota House or Senate's bills were debated—the senate bill didn't survive its committee hearing, and the house bill with the criminal penalties was withdrawn by its author. In Minnesota the State High School League already has policies for students to play sports aligned with their gender identity. Gender Justice, a Minnesota advocacy organization that works on gender issues across the country, actively fought both bills. Jess Braverman, who works with Gender Justice, says that "it's just really despicable that politicians would play games with children's lives like this. . . . There is no reason why it should be harder to play girls' kickball in Minnesota than it should be to play an Olympic elite sport."

Transgender female athlete and student NG says, "For us to sit here and criminalize those who are trying to figure out who they are, it's just ridiculous."

NG's dad adds, "It's hurtful for one thing, but it's genuinely dangerous."

The precedent for these laws was unleashed by DeVos when she withdrew the "Dear Colleague" Title IX guidance about transgender students issued by Obama's administration. However, Biden's administration has made it clear that transgender students should be able to play sports according to their gender identity rather than their sex assigned at birth. When Biden signed his executive order, he stated, "Children should be able to learn without worrying about whether they will be denied access to the restroom, the locker room, or school sports."

Education secretary Cardona has also supported transgender girls playing sports that fit their gender identity. In his confirmation hearing, Cardona said, "I think that it's critically important to have education systems and educators respect the rights of all students, including students who are transgender, and that they are afforded the opportunities that every other student has to participate in extracurricular activities."

These concentrated efforts to limit the rights of transgender girl athletes led to two opposing actions from professional women in sports. First, in December 2020, almost two hundred women athletes—including Billie Jean King, Megan Rapinoe, and WNBA legend Candace Parker—provided their support to transgender women and girls wishing to play sports. Along with Athlete Ally and the Women's Sports Foundation, the athletes signed an amicus brief. It was filed by Lambda Legal in the Ninth Circuit US Court of Appeals, to support overturning the Idaho law keeping transgender girls from sports participation.

Then, in January 2021, saying they had been studying the issue for two years, the Women's Sports Policy Working Group announced a proposal for making space in women's sport for transgender women while protecting girls' and women's rights to their sports. The group includes tennis legend Martina Navratilova and three women who used to be part of the Women's Sports Foundation—started by Billie Jean King, one of the cosigners to the amicus brief—Donna de Varona, Nancy Hogshead-Makar, and Donna Lopiano. Hogshead-Makar and Lopiano have often been consultants on Title IX legal cases. The group has no trans women members, though they claimed to consult with both trans groups and trans women professional athletes. Claiming that a middle position exists, the group's mission statement argues, "We reject both the effort to exclude trans girls and trans women from girls' and women's sport and the effort to disadvantage females by forcing them to compete against athletes with male sex-linked physical advantages."

Athlete Ally opposes the working group: "The proposals put forward . . . would only further stigmatize and isolate transgender youth at a time when they most need inclusion, access, and compassion."

Do trans girls and women dominate their sports? Do they have a competitive advantage as "athletes with male sex-linked physical advantages," as the working group claims? No. Few trans athletes have made it to the Olympics in eighteen years, even though they've been eligible for Olympic competition since 2003. Women's collegiate sports have continued uninterrupted since trans women have been allowed to play on NCAA teams. The fear that trans women have an unfair sporting advantage is probably the largest misconceptions the public has about trans women athletes. Athletic ability for trans women varies just as it does for cisgender athletes. More factors influence athletic success besides genetics—as an example, money and time spent on training also matter.

In 2019 trans writer and activist Brynn Tannehill broke down the prejudices against trans women athletes. Tannehill claims that the length of time trans women athletes have been able to compete in both the Olympics and the NCAA serves as its own longitudinal study. If we can't name any dominant trans women athletes from this time, then the current system is working: removing an athlete's testosterone for at least a year destroys any competitive advantage from the substance.

Tannehill says that sports leagues ban substances or objects (aluminum bats, for example) that provide a competitive advantage. They don't ban the people who use them. Current athletic policy has "thoroughly field tested the hypothesis that transgender athletes will dominate if they are allowed to compete, and statistically we can reject this hypothesis with [a] high degree of certainty."

In February 2021, Utah governor Spencer Cox refused to sign a

# GRACE WALKER, TRANSGENDER ATHLETE

Minnesota high school senior Grace Walker (not her real name) created this testimony for the Minnesota legislature in the spring of 2021, arguing against the state's anti-transgender legislation. Because of COVID-19, she was unable to speak to them in person, so it was posted online. This is part of her statement:

> For me, sports was a place to hang with my friends and be part of a team. I learned the values of teamwork and self-discipline. I worked hard, and after a few years I was made captain—and not because I'm the best one on the team; my athletic abilities put me squarely in the middle of the pack. My team picked me to be captain because, to be honest, I put in the work and people really like me.
>
> I'm tremendously lucky—I was never challenged to prove that I had the right to play, and that's a luxury not everyone has. But there was always this anxiety that at any moment, I'd have to justify myself to adults I don't know, to show them my personal medical forms and say, "No, I belong here. I do. This is my team. This is where I can be myself."
>
> For transgender girls like me, who have been playing sports alongside their classmates for years and who should

bill designed to keep trans girls from participating in K-12 sports. Cox was visibly emotional while talking about the bill: "These kids are . . . they're just trying to stay alive. . . . When you spend time with these kids, it changes your heart in important ways, and so I want to try to improve that message and see if we can't find a better way to work together." Though emotions are high on both sides and the road may be long, trans women athletes of all ages will continue to gain ground.

be focusing on practice like everyone else, [this bill] is a terrible reminder that we could have it all taken away. We could lose all we've worked for, our futures, our friends, and be targeted just for being who we are.

The amount of time I spend wondering if this could all end is crippling. It's nerve-wracking, and it's scary. But what's always giving me comfort and hope are my sports, tennis and cheer. When I would walk into my high school wearing my cheer uniform, I was so proud. I knew I belonged. That's a feeling every kid deserves to have. That's what high school should be about!

If lawmakers want to talk about supporting girls' and women's sports, then let's have that conversation. There are real problems in girls' and women's sports—racism, sexism, abuse, pay disparities and lack of educational opportunities, to name a few. The problem is, the only time some lawmakers talk about girls and women, it involves putting someone else down. If they'd actually like to support girls and women in sports, they can—with funding, and resources, and by weeding out predatory coaches. Nothing is stopping lawmakers from supporting girls and women's sports if that's what they really want to do. But stop using one marginalized group as a prop to harm another. It's hurtful, and it avoids the actual issues.

# CHAPTER 4

# How We Move to Equity and Equality for Women's Sports

Humans have been watching sports since the original Olympics and probably before that. Sports are part of life, just as sexism is. Moving beyond sexism is an enormous task—one that belongs to all US athletes—and it's one we have to work on if we're going to gain equity and equality for women's sports.

To begin the work, we must first consider our standards of measurement for "successful" sports teams and "successful" athletes. Do our standards of measurement even include women? We should consider these questions:

- What do we mean when we say a "popular" sport? Popular with whom? Does one audience of fans matter more than another?

- How do we define a "moneymaking" sport? How much money does a sport need to make? Enough to pay the bills? Enough to pay their athletes multiple millions in salaries?
- Are high-paid athletes the "best" athletes, or do they just get paid the most? Are standards for "best athlete" applied equitably across all genders and paid equitably?
- What are our standards for a "strong athlete"? Do we have only one standard (men with a lot of muscles)? Are women included in our definitions of "strong"?
- Do we label the grit, sweat, and effort women put into their sports as "unladylike"?
- How do other factors like race, sexuality, and disability make a difference in how we view women athletes? Do these identities make us even more likely to ignore women athletes?

If we continue to use men's athletics and men athletes as our standards of measure, women will never be fairly evaluated or supported. Eradicating stereotypes and expanding our measurements to move into equity and equality will benefit all athletes, not just women.

The ideas in this chapter may seem new or suspicious to you. They may even seem impossible, because they require such large changes. Even though many obstacles exist in this fight, these kinds of changes are entirely possible—provided people *want* the change.

Defeating sexism in women's sports can't happen without the support of both women and men, and without the support of men's college and professional sports.

We can do several things to move toward equity and equality for women's sports and women athletes.

## WOMEN UMPIRES IN MINOR-LEAGUE BASEBALL

Bernice Shiner Gera was raised in a baseball-loving family but didn't get the idea to umpire a baseball game until she was a married woman. When she signed up for the Florida Baseball School in 1967, they had no accommodations for her, and she had to live in a motel. Once she was finished with her training, she was rejected for umping positions because the National Association of Baseball Leagues argued she didn't meet the physical requirements of the job.

Gera filed a sex discrimination suit against the NABL in 1969, citing Title VII of the Civil Rights Act. She was in court with the NABL for five years, and finally won the right to umpire in January 1972. In April 1972 she was hired to umpire a doubleheader in a Class A minor league, between the Geneva Senators and the Auburn Twins. Gera quit in between games because of the lack of cooperation from the male umpires.

On January 24, 1972, *Time* noted Gera's struggles in a section called "American Notes," with the short article "The Lady Ump." According to *Time*, using language very much of its time, "Last week the New York State Court of Appeals batted 1.000 for Women's Lib by affirming the right of Mrs. Bernice Gera, a Queens housewife, to employment as a professional baseball umpire."

## EQUAL EXPOSURE

A significant way we could move toward equality in women's sports would be to promote women's sports in our media—whether the medium is television, radio, newspapers, magazines, or social media. Most people don't know women have major sports leagues or organizations in football,

Gera (*left*) calls a player safe during a Catholic Youth Organization baseball game in 1968.

Major League Baseball has employed a few female umpires, but none have worked a major-league game. Because there is an apprenticeship model for major-league umpires, all umpires must start in the minors (as Gera did), and work their way up. The timeline for that apprenticeship is long. Jen Pawol, the seventh woman ever to umpire in professional baseball and one of two working now, hopes she can ump a major-league game within five years.

basketball, soccer, softball, hockey, roller derby, tennis, bowling, and golf—most people also don't know women are paid to play their sports in football, softball, ice hockey, basketball, and soccer. Why? Fifty years after the passage of Title IX, it's still rare to see these games and matches on broadcast or cable television channels.

In fact, TV coverage of women's sports has declined. Researchers say that the decline could be because some women's sports were relegated to the "ticker" at the bottom of ESPN channels—the ticker was considered enough inclusion for women's sports, even though they were literally at the margins of the screen. Researchers also speculated that the decline of coverage has been tied to societal calls for treating women as humans rather than objects. If women athletes couldn't be a punch line or a sexy photo, networks may have decided they weren't worth covering.

A common complaint for sports fans is "women's sports are boring." Is that complaint popular because fans aren't exposed to women's sports? A small study done with college students in 2017 indicates that attitudes can be changed by exposure. After three weeks of exposure, the study found prejudices about women athletes had changed, though participant attitudes didn't change about women's sports as a whole. The only way we can judge a flexible concept like "boring" is to compare equal elements of men's and women's sports. According to Cheryl Cooky, a gender and sports researcher from Purdue, women's sports will always be judged more "boring" because of how they're covered in the media: "Men's sports are going to seem more exciting. . . . They have higher production values, higher-quality coverage, and higher-quality commentary. . . . When you watch women's sports, and there are fewer camera angles, fewer cuts to shot, fewer instant replays, yeah, it's going to seem to be a slower game, it's going to seem to be less exciting."

The Tucker Center for Research on Girls & Women in Sport at the University of Minnesota produced a documentary in 2013 about media coverage and female athletes. The center's research has found, over more than twenty years of studying media coverage, that women's sports get about 4 percent of media coverage, even though women make up 40 percent of the country's athletes. In those same longitudinal studies, the portrayal of women athletes has appeared in three primary ways: away from their playing field, out of their sports uniform, and in suggestive or sexual poses. Those three primary ways are, of course, not representative of women actually playing sports and showcasing their athletic strengths and talents. The documentary also notes that generating interest in women's sports and providing media exposure for women's sports is a complex relationship—exposure builds the fan base of women's sports, which in turn should lead to more exposure, even though the exposure is often held back because media outlets think fans aren't interested.

One of the voices in the documentary is Margaret "Digit" Murphy, then the head coach of the Boston Blades, the only women's professional hockey team in the US in 2013. The team played in the now-defunct Canadian Women's Hockey League and was known as the Worcester Blades before the league folded in 2019. The Boston Blades were the first expansion team for the league. Murphy coached the team to their victory in the 2013 Clarkson Cup. Murphy describes her experiences with the media during the victory: "We were on television nationwide in Canada. The media coverage in the paper was amazing, the Toronto Globe and Mail, like, all sorts of Canadian newspapers picked us up, I mean, we were rockstars. And then, we come home to Boston and no one even knows that we played. So, you know, it's an interesting dynamic, and I just think it really speaks to the culture of women's athletic coverage in the media."

The documentary does note how difficult it is for women athletes to be taken seriously if they choose not to be part of a sexy ad campaign. Young women seeing those sexualized images of athletes receive the message that sex is the way to get somewhere in sports. The positive skills gained from playing sports are lost, because endorsement and exposure follow the "sexy babes." While a feminist argument can be made for women being proud of their bodies and showing them off, individuals in the documentary questioned why the athleticism isn't routinely featured instead. Instead, women athletes have to be women first, rather than athletes first, and while individual athletes might benefit, women's sports as a whole does not. Tucker Center director Nicole LaVoi said, "Female athletes obviously have agency to choose how they're portrayed, but when your choices are limited and you're rarely asked to be portrayed at all, when you are, your choice is 'I could make money and be portrayed in sexualized ways' or be portrayed and make no money, that's a difficult choice . . . those choices are tempered by the lack of coverage in general."

Streaming has been very useful for increasing coverage for women's sports. It may be changing the equation. ESPN+ streamed over seven thousand hours of women's sports in 2019. With streaming platforms on the rise, including ones dedicated exclusively to sports, women's sports will provide the content the platforms need to satisfy their subscribers. ESPN has a collegiate sports television channel as well—ACC Network—and they've broadcast collegiate women's soccer, volleyball, and field hockey.

The newsletter Power Plays, written by sports journalist Lindsay Gibbs, says that women's sports were essentially forgotten at the beginning of the COVID-19 pandemic. According to Gibbs and her research assistants, "Women's sports stories only accounted for 7 percent of the sports coverage in six major newspapers during the month of May, and less than .2 percent of the non-talkshow programming on ESPN and ESPN2 combined." During May 2020, ESPN broadcast no documentaries about women and replayed no women's games. They did, however, show twenty hours of cornhole, the lawn game where competitors throw beanbags at tilted boards with holes in them. One of the ESPN networks, ESPNU, did devote 37.3 percent of its air time to women's games.

**Japan and Germany play in a woman's wheelchair basketball game in August 2021 in the Tokyo 2020 Paralympic Games.**

The COVID-19 pandemic also created some extra viewership for the WNBA. In the summer of 2020, viewership of the WNBA rose 68 percent. Will that viewership stay up when there are more sports to watch besides women's basketball? Hard to say. Did the WNBA gain some fans, thanks to their COVID season? Undoubtedly yes.

Writer Shira Springer says that we can do many things to encourage women's sports coverage, and some media outlets have already started doing it, notably espnW. Since its launch in 2010, espnW has been offering quality journalism about women's sports, with everything from statistics and long-form interviews and stories about players and teams to coverage of player workouts and slideshows. Along with espnW, Springer says we have many other ways we can provide better coverage for women athletes and their sports: "To create an environment where women's sports and women's sports coverage are valued, reporters, editors, players, coaches, academics, and others need to challenge the sometimes blatantly sexist, sometimes ignorantly biased culture that persists in sports media. It can be done through publishing great stories about women, raising awareness on social media, hiring more women, making an unapologetically feminist sports podcast, supporting new websites that give platforms to women's sports and female journalists, publicly calling out news organizations on their lack of diversity, producing academic studies that highlight gender inequality, and prominently featuring women's sports coverage."

To address the intersectional oppression faced by women athletes with disabilities, the 2021 Paralympic Games had prime-time coverage, along with more hours of coverage. The Paralympics are held after the Olympics, in the same venues. NBCUniversal announced the decision in February 2021, ahead of the August-September time frame of the Paralympics. Coverage was scheduled to include at least twelve

## JUST WOMEN'S SPORTS

In 2020 former All-Pac-12 soccer midfielder Haley Rosen founded the website and media brand Just Women's Sports, starting out "with an Instagram account and a big idea."Rosen was frustrated with the lack of coverage for women athletes and their *careers*— Rosen had admired Mia Hamm but had no way to follow the events of her playing life. As she says, "[Hamm] inspired a whole generation of female soccer players to change their lives through sport. **But what type of impact might she and her teammates have had if they had actually been given a consistent platform?** [bold in the original] How many more athletes could she have inspired if they'd been able to follow her career? If her sport hadn't been treated as a once-every-four-years event?"

Rosen says this about her new company and platform:

> Female athletes partake in [the ups and downs and drama of sport] while also having to navigate the unique complexities of being a woman in the world of sports. From dealing with condescending questions from reporters to returning to play

hundred hours of broadcast time over three different NBC channels, plus streaming and live digital platform time. The broadcasts featured top stories and big moments, plus interviews and feature stories of Paralympic athletes, focused on Team USA.

NBCUniversal also made both the Olympic and Paralympic Games more accessible by providing closed captioning for digital livestreams of events, along with the traditional closed captioning of all events on NBC's broadcast and cable networks. Closed captioning is essential for individuals who are deaf or hard of hearing. The company also made live audio descriptions available for Olympic events in prime

after childbirth, from pay disparity to hyper-sexualized media coverage, these women are competing with more than just each other to prove themselves as athletes. **Their very existence challenges the way women are perceived in society today.** [bold in the original]

For decades, female athletes have been fighting for better coverage on existing platforms. At this point, we're done holding our breath.

We're launching Just Women's Sports because we know this lack of coverage isn't just an inconvenient reality inherited from the past—it's a barrier that's actively hindering the growth of women's sports.

We're done waiting for the old platforms to catch up. We're building our own.

The company has a staff of twelve. The website features news stories about all kinds of women's sports, including specific sections for national leagues and international events and teams. It also includes a "sports ticker" at the top of its page, featuring scores and information from across the women's sports world.

time—provided by "skilled voices describing Olympic and Paralympic scenes and context"—and all Paralympic broadcast events. Live audio description is critical for blind or visually impaired spectators.

With more exposure, women's sports and women athletes probably will make more money for their advertisers and sell more tickets to their events. All forms of media need to cover women athletes and their sports as competitive and engaging, while staying away from only featuring them for their beauty or their bodies. If media can sustain that coverage, there are no bad outcomes from more exposure for women's athletes and women's sports.

## EQUAL MONEY AND ACCESS

Women professional athletes get paid much less than their male counterparts. While women's salaries definitely need to change—Steph Curry's $40 million salary in 2019 was more than three times the $12.5 million salaries of *all* WNBA players—equity and equality also apply to travel accommodations, access to marketing, and many other elements of the financial powerhouse that is American sports culture. Sports money and sports marketing is a boys' club, and letting women in to that chamber would upset the privilege men have held for as long as America has had sports.

In January 2020, the WNBA made some strides in this fight. Players agreed to an eight-year collective-bargaining agreement (player contract) that provided serious gains in several areas. The top players' salaries almost doubled, and performance incentives were added. Marketing money was significantly increased, as were flight and travel accommodations. Family benefits were also added, including paid maternity leave, money for childcare, and a reimbursement for surrogacy or fertility treatments. Players also gained better mental health benefits. A provision for job opportunities after women are finished playing the WNBA was added. The gains made by the WNBA players leave a positive legacy for future players.

Team bubbles created for the NBA and the WNBA in the summer of 2020 during COVID-19 weren't equal. The NBA stayed in a posh hotel on the Disney World property, with luxurious food from a culinary staff, personally prepared to individual players' needs. The WNBA stayed in condos, with some meals provided. The NBA men had access to barbers, players-only lounges with gaming, and fun excursions. The WNBA women didn't. Yes, Disney and the NBA have a relationship (Disney owns ABC and ESPN, and those channels broadcast NBA games), so both help the other make money, but ESPN also holds the broadcast rights to the WNBA, and they have thus far chosen to give the league less air time.

As you read in chapter 3, the US women's national soccer team is still fighting for equal pay. They're still more popular and have more titles than the men but are paid much less. According to Megan Rapinoe, "A top-tier women's national team player would earn

## Vicious Cycle of Marketing in Women's Sports

lower revenue

less marketing and promotion for women's teams

fewer opportunities to develop fan base

less interest from sponsors

Systemic sexism creates a vicious cycle when it comes to marketing in women's sports. Organizers must actively invest in promotion and marketing for women's teams and athletes in order to build their popularity.

38 percent of the compensation of her equivalent of the men's teams."

WNBA superstar (and Rapinoe's fiancée) Sue Bird says, "When I think of pay equity, I think of the opportunity that the NBA and other male sports leagues have to be successful." How would that kind of equity look for the super-popular US women's national soccer team?

According to sports writer Anya Alvarez, marketing and promotion

## WOMEN WHO OWN SPORTS TEAMS

Not many women own professional sports teams. Sports team ownership is often by groups, where all the individuals in the group aren't public, so it's hard to create an accurate count of women team owners. In the NFL (thirty-two teams) and the NBA (thirty teams), the number of women owners appears to be under ten for each league. In the National Hockey League, the number appears to be under three. It appears no current Major League Baseball owners are women, though the first woman to own a baseball team was Helene Britton, who inherited the St. Louis Cardinals in March 1911 from her uncle. Team ownership passing from family member to family member is a common way women become team owners. In 2019 Jane Skinner Goodell debuted the film *A Lifetime of Sundays* that chronicles four women NFL owners who are part of football legacy families: Virginia Halas McCaskey (Chicago Bears), Patricia Rooney (Pittsburgh Steelers), Norma Hunt (Kansas City Chiefs), and Martha Ford (Detroit Lions). Sheila Ford Hamp leads the Detroit Lions, taking over for her mother in 2020.

Fewer than five women own WNBA teams, a league that makes no secret of its support for equity and justice. Kelly Loeffler, a former Republican US senator from Georgia and the former owner of the Atlanta Dream, came under fire for admonishing the WNBA for supporting the Black Lives Matter movement. The issues may be even more important parts of the equation than equal pay. Systemic sexism helps determine how much marketing and promotion is done for women's teams and women athletes, and not having any marketing means not having ways to build a fan base, thus not building revenue for the team. No marketing means no foundation for players and teams to build interest and attract sponsors.

Sheila Ford Hamp (*left*) has been part of the Detroit Lions management team since her mother took over the team in 2014. She became the principal owner of the team in 2020.

league displayed "Black Lives Matter" on its basketball courts in the summer of 2020. Members of her team immediately distanced themselves from her and began wearing T-shirts to support her opponent and eventual winner of the Senate election, Raphael Warnock, who is Black. In January 2021, the team was sold to two real estate executives and former Atlanta Dream player Renee Montgomery. The sale demonstrated that politics and sports are partners, and the era of players following the "shut up and dribble" rule is over for the WNBA.

In the National Women's Soccer League, more women owners have become part of the league. The Angel City Football Club in Los Angeles has at least thirty women who are partial owners. Their majority ownership group is led by actor Natalie Portman, along with two other women and a man. Tennis legend Serena Williams is a partial owner, as are fourteen former members of the US women's national soccer team.

Equal marketing and promotion is key. Washington Mystics player Elena Delle Donne summed up the problems, saying, "When you put millions of dollars into marketing athletes and allowing fans to get to know a player they develop a connection with someone or something you are more engaged and continue to want to see/learn more. How is anyone going to get to know me or any of my colleagues if we aren't marketed as much?"

Colleges will also need to grapple with how they will share revenues from the names, images, and likenesses of college athletes. The conversation about NIL compensation heated up in 2020 and 2021 and will likely take a few more years to sort out. An Associated Press survey of ninety-nine college athletic directors, completed in April 2021, said that many of them worry these compensation rules will hurt women's sports. If generated revenue must be used to pay these athletes, no money will be left to support women's programs, which (according to stereotypes) make no money for a college. Gender was not part of the survey data, but as a reference point, only 14 percent of athletic directors in Division I programs are women.

Even though there's a long way to go, marketing trends may be shifting toward equity. Before the COVID-19 pandemic, women's college basketball ticket prices were climbing, thanks to excellent college players and competitive, exciting games. If tickets are hot commodities, and they cost as much or more than men's tickets, the perceived value of the sport goes up. Also important is a generational shift about who is "allowed" to be a women's sports fan. Gender equity sports researcher Nancy Lough, from the University of Nevada, Las Vegas, noted that 84 percent of sports fans in her research support women's sports. According to sports marketer Joe Favorito, "We've now reached a generation where it's not just OK, but it's really not unexpected that, no matter if you are a man, woman, boy or girl, if you want to go see quality athletes, some of those quality athletes that you can root for may be women."

Female athletes are also making their own decisions about sponsorships. Some are even leaving powerhouse Nike for brands that feel more appropriate to their careers and legacies. Superstar Olympic gymnast Simone Biles left Nike for Athleta, a Gap brand and a label directed toward women, as did Olympic gold medalist runner Allyson Felix. According to Allison Galer, founder of Disrupt the Game, a sports agency that works exclusively with women, "Female athletes have to do what's best for them at all times . . . [b]ecause they don't get to have the cushion of millions of millions of dollars that they're making [in their sport]."

Basketball superstar and Olympian Breanna Stewart signed with Puma because the company was willing to make her a signature shoe. Stewart said, "Women basketball players deserve to have signature shoes."

Felix's sponsorship story is emblematic of a major problem professional female athletes face: how to fit motherhood into a sports career and sports sponsorship. When Felix became pregnant, she was renegotiating her sponsorship with Nike. Because of her pregnancy, Nike planned to reduce her salary by 70 percent. Felix left Nike for Athleta and started her own shoe brand called Saysh. Shoes were available for preorder as of August 2021. The shoes are specifically designed for women's feet. Felix sees Saysh as part of the legacy she plans to build after she's done running; "If I can bring about some change and create this [shoe company] in a way that I believe it should be built, and do something for women, to me that's still having a say, and having a voice."

## WOMEN ATHLETES AND WOMEN'S SPORTS NEED EQUAL SUPPORT

If we want to show women athletes their equity and equality matters, we need to support them in every way. Equal exposure and equal money generation are two ways to do it, but we also must support them with everything from equal facilities and equipment to equal representation in sports history. We must also mentor women and girl athletes to know and demand their power.

During the spring 2021 annual college basketball playoffs for men and women—only men's teams are allowed to call it March Madness—various viral videos and posts showed the nation the double standards the NCAA perpetuates between men's and women's sports. The exposure began with University of Oregon player Sedona Prince's instantly iconic post about the paltry weight room facilities for the women's basketball teams compared to the thoroughly supplied weight room for the men's basketball teams. Several other players

Prince is eager to use her voice to amplify issues for women in the NCAA. "It's so amazing that now I have such a big platform," she said. "I'm able to inspire and help so many people and bring so much attention to my sport, because that's what it deserves."

and coaches criticized the disparity, with some of the harshest commentary coming from a note shared on Twitter by University of Georgia coach Nell Fortner. Fortner started with "Thank you for using the three biggest weeks of your organization's year to expose how you feel about women's basketball—an afterthought." Fortner pointed out many differences between the men's and women's treatment at the tournaments and ended with this thought, "For too long, women's basketball has accepted an attitude and treatment from the NCAA that has been substandard in its championships. It's time for this to stop. It's time for women's basketball to receive the treatment it has earned." After the public shaming from both the posts and the media, the NCAA apologized and vowed to do better.

Mark Emmert, president of the NCAA, commissioned a report to study and compare the college men's and women's national basketball tournaments after he was accused of downplaying concerns of players and coaches. Roberta Kaplan and her law firm, specializing in civil rights, released the report in August 2021. The report found the spending gap between the tournaments was about $35 million, including advertising, sponsorship, food for players, and venue transformations. The disparity in allocation has been in effect for years. Kaplan's report says that the "fundamental difference in perspective about the relative importance of the 2021 men's and women's championships led to gender disparities from the very outset of the planning process." The report offered more than twenty-five suggestions for improvement.

The Women's Sports Foundation has been studying girls and women in sports for more than twenty-five years. According to their research, at least six factors cause girls to feel unsupported enough to drop out of sports after the age of fourteen. First are a lack of opportunities both in school and outside it (including a lack of facilities) and a lack of safe transportation to suburban sports facilities for girls in dense urban areas. Bullying and social stigma, especially around the stereotype of "all girls who play sports are gay," and a decrease in having quality sports experiences, thanks to a lack of coaches, facilities, equipment, and playing times, also contribute to girls dropping out. Sports just stop being fun. Finally, girls also drop out because of costs and a lack of positive role models that demonstrate strength and enjoyment of physical activity, rather than external beauty. These discrepancies are even greater for girls of color. According to the National Women's Law Center, Black and Latina girls play sports less often than their white classmates, and immigrant girls play sports at less than half the rate of immigrant boys.

# QUESTIONABLE SUPPORT IN TOKYO

The 2020 Tokyo Olympics, held in 2021, were the first Olympics where the numbers of male and female competitors were almost equal—which was big news. However, the support exhibited for women competitors was still questionable. Canadian boxer Mandy Bujold was initially disqualified from competing. Because of the pandemic, qualification matches were evaluated in 2018 and 2019, when Bujold was pregnant and then caring for her infant daughter. She appealed her disqualification to the Court of Arbitration for Sport and won.

Another motherhood issue was raised for Canadian basketball player Kim Gaucher. Because of COVID restrictions, her breastfeeding daughter was initially not going to be allowed in the Olympic Village. The baby girl was considered an "unaccredited person," and the village is only open to athletes and athletic personnel. Gaucher was being asked to choose between her daughter and her Olympic career. Thanks to mounting public pressure and Gaucher's continued appeals, the decision was reversed.

Possibly these kinds of "difficult issues" wouldn't be difficult if more women were part of the International Olympic Committee. In 2021 women were 33.3 percent of the executive board, and 37.5 percent of the committee members. No woman has ever been a president of the IOC.

According to the Representation Project, which studies gender in media, in the first week of the Tokyo Olympics, women received almost 60 percent of the prime-time coverage—a truly surprising figure. However, the commentators for the Olympics are still 82 percent men, and men are still seen as the "default" athlete— "female" athletes were named as such 13.6 percent of the time, while "male" athletes were named only 2 percent of the time. Women athletes were seven times more likely to be referred to as a "girl" or other term that could feminize or infantilize them.

The Representation Project did report a few positives: "Women athletes received more coverage than men athletes. We find no gender gaps in discussions of romantic partners, marital status, parenting, appearance, or body shaming."

Sexism also showed itself during the coverage of street skateboarder Alana Smith. They are the first out non-binary athlete to compete for any US Olympic team. During broadcast coverage of their event, Smith was misgendered when the broadcasters used the wrong pronouns for them. The broadcasters apologized. Outsports said, "It isn't hard to correctly gender an athlete. Knowing such information falls into the purview of a commentator's job."

**Smith smiled throughout their run at the 2020 Olympic Games. In an Instagram post, they expressed their thankfulness for being able to represent the non-binary community on an international stage.**

Changing any or all of these six factors could increase support for girls of all colors in sports. These changes would also provide more of the positive benefits that sports bring to girls and young women, including more responsible behavior, better health, stronger academic achievement, better mental health, and potentially better jobs after high school and college, due to better teamwork skills.

Making sure girls and women see themselves represented in sports history—from "firsts" to "great moments"—will also signal support. The Pro Football Hall of Fame, in Canton, Ohio, logs visitors every year from all fifty states and many foreign countries, with more than ten million in-person visitors since the museum opened in 1963. Where is the National Hall of Fame for Professional Women's Sports? Even though the All-American Girls Professional Baseball League has its own feature in the National Baseball Hall of Fame and Museum, in Cooperstown, New York, currently no sports museum exists to showcase any other women's sports achievements. That may soon change. Sue Zipay, who played baseball with the Rockford Peaches as part of the All-American Girls Professional Baseball League in the 1950s, began organizing the effort to create the Women's Sports Museum in 2015 in Sarasota, Florida. The museum has a board of directors and a national marketing campaign (phase 1), and is in phase 2 of its plan, including a fundraising campaign and a preview center in the Mall at University Town Center in Sarasota, to showcase some of the history that will be included in the museum. They hope to begin phase 3—site selection and museum construction—by 2023.

Mentors could make a big difference in supporting girls in sports. According to researchers Kathryn Vaggalis and Margaret Kelley, it can even help girls fight both sexism and sexual harassment by showing girls they matter—and they don't have to accept poor treatment from others. Their study found mentoring is key to helping girls feel seen and heard, but it can also boost athletic performance and provide the desire to continue in sports. Vaggalis and Kelley's research was done with college students who played sports in high school, both men and women. The students identified mentors where the relationship had arisen naturally, such as with teachers or coaches, rather than mentors who had been assigned to them. Even though the research regarding mentoring girls was positive, men reported mentoring experiences that reinforced traditional masculine stereotypes related to sports—not much emotional support, not much open communication—though the focus on sports performance was helpful to them. These traditional forms of sports masculinity can reinforce the idea that sports are a masculine domain. The researchers argue their findings are, again, a good reminder to examine how we treat boys and girls, so everyone can gain the benefits of a positive, open relationship with a mentor.

At the University of Tennessee, the Center for Sport, Peace and Society administers a unique and powerful idea for global mentoring. In collaboration with espnW and the US Department of State, center director Sarah Hillyer runs the Global Sports Mentoring Program. The program brings in women already in the sports industry from across the globe to work with American sports organizations and senior women within those organizations. Program participants must be nominated by the US embassy in their country, and they must have several years' experience in a sports-based organization, often one that focuses on girls and women.

The Global Sports Mentoring Program website says that girls' and women's participation in sports can lead to "social and economic empowerment," because participants develop new networks, gain self-esteem and a strong identity, and engage differently in their world. Encouraging girls and women around the globe to play sports also boosts leadership skills and participation in decision-making, along with working to destroy sexist stereotypes and discrimination. The program believes that women practicing these skills across cultural and country boundaries will make the world stronger.

# WOMEN COACHES

Women have to fight to become coaches in any league. Sexist double standards exist about their behavior and their communication styles—women coaches are "abusive" and "demeaning," but men are "passionate" and "tough." Gender stereotypes ask women to be more motherly and kind but certainly not antagonistic or difficult. Women coaches are punished for acting like stereotypical men, punished for not acting like them, and punished for acting like stereotypical women. The percentage of female coaches has actually fallen since Title IX became US law.

Women coaches might matter most at the K–12 level, when they are actively influencing young women athletes. MM, a high school athlete (tennis, volleyball, softball) from a small town in the Midwest, says, "The relationship of athlete to coach is more important than the record or the wins or losses of the team. Women coaches have had similar aspirations to the players, so they know where the players are. They can support players in ways beneficial to women players—men don't know what women need. Women are also able to deal with drama and conflicts in a way that's relatable to women. We have three female varsity head coaches out of twenty coaches in our district. That's not enough."

MM also says that male coaches are common in women's sports, even if they haven't played the sport themselves: "Why is it so normalized [to have] male coaches in volleyball, and softball? These male coaches have never played these sports competitively, but yet they have a say in what the players should do in order to play the sport successfully. How can they give us points and tips on how to get better at a sport they have never played before? Even if the male coach has done tons of research and outside work to learn more about the sport, they haven't ever physically participated in that sport and been in a woman's body."

In March 2019 then Notre Dame head women's basketball coach Muffet McGraw was thinking along similar lines. McGraw announced she would no longer hire male coaches for her program. According to

McGraw, "Girls are socialized to know . . . that gender roles are already set. Men run the world. Men have the power. Men make the decisions. . . . When these girls are coming out, who are they looking up to telling them that's not the way it has to be? And where better to do that than in sports?"

As general manager for the Miami Marlins, Kim Ng is currently the highest-ranking women baseball executive in MLB.

Women have to fight even harder to become coaches in men's professional leagues, but more are being hired every day. In January 2021 Jennifer King became the first full-time Black female coach with the Washington Football Team. King is an assistant coach for their running backs. Elsewhere in the NFL, Lori Locust is an assistant defensive line coach and Maral Javadifar is an assistant strength coach for the Tampa Bay Buccaneers. They were the first women football coaches to win a Super Bowl title. Katie Sowers was an offensive assistant coach for the San Francisco 49ers. She was the first woman and first openly gay coach to coach in a Super Bowl. In the summer of 2021, Sowers began coaching with the Kansas City Chiefs.

In Major League Baseball, Kim Ng (Miami Marlins) became the first woman in North America to be hired as a general manager in November 2020. Five other women have full-time roles in MLB—Amanda Hopkins (Seattle Mariners), Justine Siegal (Oakland Athletics), Rachel Balkovec (New York Yankees), Rachel Folden (Chicago Cubs), and Alyssa Nakken (San Francisco Giants). Balkovec changed her name on her résumé from Rachel to Rae so men's teams wouldn't discard her application.

In the NBA, at least fifteen former WNBA players and college basketball stars have coaching and managing positions. In the National Hockey League, Dawn Braid became the first full-time woman coach when she was hired by the Arizona Coyotes, though she no longer coaches for them.

Individual sports may also issue guidance for mentoring girls. The Squash and Education Alliance, based in New York City, brings together nonprofit organizations in the US and abroad to provide support to young squash players through middle and high school into college. They created a ten-page guide covering how to mentor and care for girls in squash programs. The report includes everything from how to develop self-esteem and confidence to how to support girls who need sports bras, menstruation products, and athletic hijabs. The organization says that squash teams and clubs should "think about all aspects of your program from the perspective of access related to gender," but that considering the needs of girls to make programs equitable will provide broad results. "As we improve our programs to better serve our girls, we will by default create stronger programs for all players."

## #METOO AND WOMEN'S SPORTS

Sexual harassment and sexual abuse happen to women athletes more often than we know. Making things more equitable and equal means stopping both harassment and abuse, as well as listening to the victims of both. Girls and women must be believed when they say their rights or bodies have been violated. The hashtag "#MeToo" was started by sexual assault survivor and activist Tarana Burke in 2006, to offer solidarity to those who had survived sexual assault. The phrase came to national prominence in 2017 as media mogul Harvey Weinstein's widespread sexual abuse came to light.

One of the most repulsive cases of sexual abuse in sports involves Larry Nassar, the former team doctor for the US women's national gymnastics team. He was accused of assaulting at least 265 young women, starting in 1992, and was sentenced to 175 years in a Michigan state prison in January 2018 (with more time added later). Nassar's case is blatant abuse but is only one end of the spectrum of potentially damaging treatment of women athletes. Sexual abuse and harassment in women's sports is more common than public reporting suggests. A study conducted

Olympic gold medal gymnast Jordyn Wieber testifies before a US Senate panel regarding the sexual abuse she suffered at the hands of Larry Nassar.

in Norway in 2000 showed that of 572 elite female athletes representing fifty-eight different sports, 28 percent had been harassed by someone in authority in sports or by another athlete.

According to Christina Long, a student journalist at the University of Missouri who covers their football team, even women sports journalists have to stay aware of choices men are making. She says that teams can crack down on blatant sexual harassment, such as what was uncovered in the Washington Football Team's organization in the summer of 2020, but small things matter too: "how [men] address the women in the room, how you interact with them and uplift them or don't, how you help grow their work or don't. I feel like it's pretty easy not to harass people and assault people. It's easy to avoid the very obviously bad things, but it's the smaller things that are hard."

The damage done by sexual harassment and sexual abuse has many consequences. Women question their self-worth, and they lose trust in their surroundings and the people who are supposed to support them. How abusers cope with their consequences can also harm those previously injured again. John Geddert was a former Olympic coach for the US women's gymnastics team. In February 2021, he was charged with sexual assault, human trafficking, and other crimes related to his time working with Larry Nassar. Rather than face the consequences, Geddert took his own life. His survivors now must face the rage and frustration of never seeing their abuser held accountable for his crimes.

# KOBE AND GIANNA BRYANT

Basketball legend Kobe Bryant and his daughter Gianna were killed on January 26, 2020, in a helicopter crash. They were on their way to Bryant's basketball academy when the crash occurred. Bryant was an unwavering supporter of Gigi's basketball career, and consequently put his support behind the WNBA as well, saying right before his death that WNBA players "Diana Taurasi, Maya Moore, Elena Della Donne" could play in the NBA. In 2018 he told Jimmy Kimmel that he loved having fans say to him that he and his wife, Vanessa, needed to have a baby boy to carry on the legacy of his career. He told Kimmel, "[Gigi would say] 'I've got this. You don't need no boy for that. I've got this.' And I'm like that's right. Yes you do. You got this!" He and his daughters also supported the US women's national soccer team by attending their games. He believed having more girls and women in sports was the future of sports.

Kobe and Gianna Bryant enjoy a game between the Los Angeles Lakers and the Dallas Mavericks in December 2019.

Two other members of Gianna's basketball team were also killed in the helicopter crash: Alyssa Altobelli and Payton Chester. All three girls were honored in the 2020 WNBA draft as honorary selections to the league. Jerseys were created for them.

The WNBA also created the Kobe and Gigi Bryant WNBA Advocacy Award, to honor individuals who guide the next generation of players and give back to the basketball community.

## MEN MUST DO THEIR PART

One key element that must also be present in this work is men. They must use their privilege to promote equity and equality for women's sports and to stop other men from sexual harassment and assault of women involved in sports—athletes, staff, writers, and anyone else. Men will face opposition in this task because the patriarchy will resist their efforts. Researchers W. Brad Johnson and David G. Smith say, "Active confrontation of other men for sexism, bias, harassment, and all manner of inappropriate behavior may be the toughest part of male allyship. It is also utterly essential."

Writer Jerry Brewer argues that women are not surprised at bad behavior of men in the sports world: "For women, there is no shock, only lasting discomfort, unrelieved pain. They endure the emotional triggering and keep telling their stories of working and associating with abusive and territorial men, hoping we might pursue honest examination of the endemic sexism in sports."

Former NFL quarterback and sports researcher Don McPherson says, "We never get deep into the difficult part, which is that it's men who perpetuate the problem, even when women aren't there." McPherson adds that boys aren't raised to be men, that they're raised not to be women, which creates the breeding ground to abuse and forgets the needs of women, all under the label of "boys will be boys." McPherson argues, "Until we realize that ideology actually hurts us, there won't be the motivation to solve it. We have to realize that, while maintaining the status quo might not hurt us now, we are hurting our sons by clinging to it. They will not have the example and the methods to adapt to change."

William Broussard was an athletic administrator at four NCAA schools, including the University of Arizona (Division I) in Tucson, Centenary College (Division III) in Shreveport, Louisiana, and his alma mater, Northwestern State University of Louisiana (Division I) in Natchitoches, where Broussard had been an All-American and Academic All-American offensive lineman. During his three years as the athletic

# COACH M'S EXPERIENCES

Coach M talks about being a high school soccer player and later becoming a coach:

While a high school female soccer player in suburban Dallas, Texas in the late 80s and early 90s, I witnessed several discrepancies between female and male sports, especially football. It was clear that our school, which was located in a middle to upper class suburb in north Dallas, favored male sports over female sports. The athletic training room and weight room were essentially attached to the boys' locker room and football locker room. To get to the training room, the female athletes had to walk down a couple of hallways which constituted about half the width of the building. One entrance to the training room was in a hallway while the other led directly to the boys' locker rooms. This culture left me feeling less valuable. I didn't feel that I was being seen as a valuable contributor to the school environment. Not only did I feel that I was not an important part of our school community, I also felt that soccer was a "lesser" sport. Being a high school student with a limited vision of the world around me, I assumed that the world in general thought soccer wasn't valuable. I felt like the sport I loved and that connected me to other people was devalued.

While the parking lots were not labeled as such, it was well known that the football team parked in one particular lot. From that lot led a sidewalk which allowed players to directly enter their locker room. On the sidewalk was painted horseshoes as our mascot was the Mustang. If you parked in that lot and were not a football player (or dating one), you were likely to experience verbal reminders from members of the football team or even damage to your car. I was fortunate enough to have dated a football player for a time so it was acceptable for me to park in the lot. However, when I was not dating the football player, I knew I shouldn't park there anymore. This unspoken hierarchy generated a sense of being ranked in order of importance. If I was "important" enough, I could park there. The feeling of being ranked or compared led to some feelings of not being good enough. That's a tough place to be as a developing high school girl.

I am sure that no one intended for the imbalance of power to be this way. The plan for the building probably never considered accessibility for males and females to the athletic training room or weight room. There were no signs specifically reserving the "football lot" (as it was called) for the football team. However, no one ever did anything to change the culture or equally represent both genders. I was angry that this seemed "acceptable". Those feelings are still with me today as I reflect on my high school experiences.

After college, I came to Minnesota to teach and coach, and I began to coach a high school girls' soccer team in urban Minnesota. My experience was very different from my Texas high school. My activities director made it clear from the beginning that certain sports and genders were not more valued than others. She was a champion for equity across genders and across rosters sizes. For instance, girls' soccer and football received equal treatment just as boys swimming and football received equal treatment. Many athletes may not realize what a gift it was to participate in an equitable school environment, but I do. I know that my athletes were never left questioning their value or the value of their sport. I am proud of the environment that I coach in and am thankful that I can heal some of the anger that I carried with me from my high school experience.

director at Southern University and A&M College (Division I) in Baton Rouge, Louisiana, he focused on closing gender inequity gaps.

Southern University had a budget crisis, so Broussard raised money from athletic department supporters, increased game and ticket revenues, and rearranged money in current budgets to make his vision happen. He added scholarships for women athletes. He replaced unsuccessful male coaches of women's programs with female coaches—leading to the first conference division championship in the history of the women's soccer program and the first conference tournament championship appearance in over a decade for the women's volleyball program. He created a coaching position and hired a woman for the men's and women's cross-country team. He hired a woman as his director of sports medicine, and then hired women as trainers. The all-women staff cared for all athletic programs, including football. He also hired the only woman strength and conditioning coach who oversaw a football program along with the other programs she served—she was the only woman in Division I to do so.

Broussard's work was also intersectional, since Southern University and A&M College is a historically Black college or university (HBCU). Broussard wanted to be sure women athletes and coaches were valued more than Black women historically are, in wider American culture and in sports culture. His work, as a Black man, also signaled to other Black men that they too were welcome to add their support. He wanted all athletes and students to be proud of the gender equity and quality sports programs at Southern, and to be happy to call the school their alma mater, but keeping unfair judgment and racism away from his Black athletes was a primary goal. Broussard didn't leave Southern until 2017, but he left the athletic department in 2015. His changes didn't last. By 2020 all the women head coaches and department heads he'd hired had either been replaced by men or had had their positions eliminated.

Because the NCAA has so much power and influence, as do donors who contribute millions of dollars to individual schools,

Broussard believes change must be forced by entities outside of schools: "The pressure has to come from the outside—agitation, protest, social unrest, lobbying, engaging lawmakers. That's the only time the NCAA has made changes. There's no such thing as half justice, or half civil rights. If it means that there's not enough money, but people are going to be safe and welcome and we're going to follow the law, we gotta figure out another way to make money." Broussard also advocates teaching women to challenge the power structures of athletic departments and college sports from within, creating blueprints for women players, coaches, and staff to follow as they advocate for themselves. Those plans could be shared with women at other schools, so the pressure on the system increases each time a woman stands up for herself.

Ultimately, our US sports culture has to *decide* to make these changes, just as larger American culture must decide to change sexism. As a culture, we have to decide that "strong athletes" can be men or women. We have to prioritize exposure and advertising for women's sports, with the assumption that they'll gather even more revenue and attention as more people see them. Writer Liz Elting says, "Fighting for equal rights and equal opportunities entails risk. It demands you put yourself in harm's way by calling out injustice when it occurs. Sometimes it's big things, like a boss making overtly sexist remarks or asserting they won't hire women. But far more often, it's little, seemingly innocuous, things like spur-of-the-moment drinks that sideline the women whose work you depend on every day. You can use your privilege to help those who don't have it. It's really as simple as that."

Our US sports system, at all levels, has to say to women athletes, "We want to see you play. We're here to support you." Then we have to prove it with media time, advertising money, salaries and pay equity, representation, and changed stereotypes and attitudes.

## CHAPTER 5

# The Future of Equity and Equality for Women's Sports

**W**hat does the future look like for girls and women in sports? We can see it in our athletes, our sports officials, and in our organizations.

The future looks like tennis champion Naomi Osaka and decorated Olympic gymnast Simone Biles, who continue to push their sports forward while they also work for equitable treatment for all. In 2020 Osaka was named Female Athlete of the Year by the Associated Press, for her excellence in tennis and her racial activism off the court. Osaka does not shy away from saying what she thinks. During the 2020 US Open, Osaka wore pandemic face masks with the names of Black individuals killed by the police. Biles, who holds the most titles of any woman gymnast in the world, said in 2019 that women in sports must claim their achievements: "You only see the men doing it. And they're praised for it and the women are looked down upon for it. But I feel it's good [to do] because once you realize you're confident and good at it, then you're even better at what you do."

In 2021 both Osaka and Biles withdrew from prominent competitions to protect and care for their physical and mental

Osaka wore a face mask honoring Tamir Rice during the 2020 US Open. Twelve-year-old Tamir was shot and killed by a Cleveland, Ohio, police officer on November 22, 2014.

health. Osaka left the French Open, citing anxiety related to press conferences, and Biles withdrew from several parts of her planned Tokyo Olympic competition because of the "twisties," a situation where a gymnast can't control her body as she does a move. Both decisions created firestorms of controversy. Osaka's and Biles's intersectional identities made their choices even more open to criticism. Both women are Black, and Biles has ADHD. Neither woman backed away from their decisions, and their steadfastness sparked larger and necessary conversations that included intersectionality.

Writer and political consultant Marcela Howell says in an article about Biles and Osaka, "For Black women, [the challenges surrounding mental health and self-care are] doubly felt—experienced at the intersection of racial and gender oppression. The stereotype of the 'strong Black woman' was born of Black women's sheer need to persevere and be resilient in the face of staggering misogyny, racism, and the widespread economic and health disparities that result." Biles eventually returned to competition, winning a bronze medal in vault. Osaka, who was born in Osaka, Japan, was the torch lighter for the Tokyo Olympic Games. She did not medal.

In July 2021, Osaka wrote an essay for *Time*. She stated, "I feel uncomfortable being the spokesperson or face of athlete mental health as it's still so new to me and I don't have all the answers. I do hope that people can relate and understand it's OK to not be OK, and it's OK to talk about it. There are people who can help, and there is usually light at the end of any tunnel.

"Michael Phelps told me that by speaking up I may have saved a life. If that's true, then it was all worth it."

The Tokyo Olympics showed us an even broader vision for the future of women, non-binary, and LBGTQIA+ athletes. It was the first set of Olympic Games where women were almost 49 percent of the participants, and of the Paralympic athletes, with almost 41 percent women. Compared to the 2016 Rio Olympic Games, there are more than triple the number of out LGBTQIA+ athletes competing in Tokyo, with out women outnumbering out men by about eight to one. Trans woman Laurel Hubbard competed for New Zealand in weightlifting, and trans woman Chelsea Wolfe traveled to Tokyo as an alternate for the US BMX team. Non-binary soccer player Quinn won a gold medal with Team Canada. After the Olympics, the International Olympic Committee decided to reconfigure the rules for transgender and intersex athletes in order to move IOC policies closer to equity and nondiscrimination. Their choice to alter these policies is an enormous step forward.

The future looks like women athletes who are strongly tied to their communities. Eighteen-year-old gymnast Sunisa (Suni) Lee won the gold medal for the all-around gymnastics events in the 2020 Tokyo Olympics. From Saint Paul, Minnesota, Lee is the daughter of Hmong immigrants and part of one of the largest communities of Hmong refugees in the world. Her parents and her community supported her from childhood gymnastic lessons through 2021's Olympic competition. Her dad built her a balance beam for the backyard, the community held fundraisers for her, and more than three hundred people gathered in a rented event center to watch the TV footage from Tokyo. Lee said, "Right before the medal ceremony I FaceTimed my sister, and everybody in the camera was screaming and crying and I was just like, 'I did it,' and we just had this little moment where it was just like, 'We did it.'"

Indigenous Hawaiian Carissa Moore won a gold medal in surfing as a rainbow suddenly materialized in the midst of the clouds from Tropical Storm Nepartak, over the ocean where she was competing. Rainbows

**Lee is the first Hmong American Olympian. She won three medals at the 2020 Tokyo Olympic Games: gold in the all-around competition, silver in the team competition, and bronze on the uneven bars.**

are a historic symbol of the Hawaiian Islands. Indigenous Hawaiians invented the sport of surfing. One of the sport's ancestors, Duke Kahanamoku (a swimmer, winning gold and silver in the 1912 Olympics), traveled extensively to advocate for surfing's inclusion in the Olympics. That debut happened in Tokyo. The first gold medal in the sport went to Moore, from Oahu, the island where a statue of Kahanamoku stands on its most famous beach, Waikiki. Moore walked by the statue as a child learning to surf. Moore and other Hawaiian surfers will continue to ask the sports community to recognize and honor the Hawaiian roots of the sport, created long before the islands were colonized.

The future looks like women participating fully in sports that have gained status and prestige with traditionally male participants. Women's freestyle wrestling has been in the Olympics since 2004, and the Japanese women's wrestling team has dominated the sport in every weight class. The skill of their wrestlers is admired around the world. In the Tokyo Olympics, US wrestler Tamyra Mensah-Stock broke that dynasty to win a gold medal in the 68 kg (150-pound) weight class. She is the first US Black woman to win a gold medal in wrestling at

## SIMONE BILES'S GOAT LEOTARDS AND PENALIZED EXCELLENCE

In 2021 Simone Biles debuted the rhinestone outline of a goat's head on her leotard (named Goldie), symbolizing that she's the GOAT (Greatest of All Time) of women's gymnastics. Why did she put such an audacious brag on her uniform? According to Biles, "The idea was to hit back at the haters. . . . I just hope that kids growing up watching this don't or aren't ashamed at being good at whatever they do . . . everybody can say you're good, but once you acknowledge it, it's not [acceptable] anymore. And I want kids to learn that yes, it's okay to acknowledge that you're good or even great at something."

It's not just the haters who penalize Biles for being the GOAT. The International Gymnastics Federation (FIG) has undervalued some gymnastics moves only Biles can complete, giving them a lower "start value" (measure of their difficulty) than many sport experts believe they deserve. The organization made these decisions against two of Biles's elements (in floor exercise and balance beam) in the 2019 World Championships and again in the 2021 Open Championships (vault).

As Biles argued in 2019, "Am I in a league of my own? Yes? But that doesn't mean you can't credit me for what I'm doing. . . . They keep asking us to do more difficulty and to give more the Olympics. The Tokyo Olympics were also the first time women competed in canoeing, and nineteen-year-old American woman Nevin Harrison received the first gold medal in the sport.

These athletes succeeding in previously male-dominated sports also keep getting younger. US park skateboarder Brighton Zeuner was seventeen when she competed in Tokyo, and she thought she was old—but street skateboard medalists Momiji Nishiya (gold) and Rayssa Leal (silver) can't drive yet. Zeuner's top competitors in

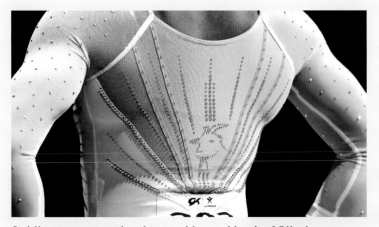

Goldie appears on the sleeves, hip, and back of Biles's competitive leotards.

artistry, give more harder skills. . . . So we do, and then they don't credit it, and I don't think that's fair."

Sports writer Nancy Armour points out the error in the organization's thinking: "The FIG should be celebrating the unique combination of natural talent, hard work and smart training that makes Biles a once-in-a-lifetime athlete, and commending her for challenging herself and her sport. Instead, gymnastics officials are embarrassed by the massive gap Biles has opened on the rest of the field, and are throwing up artificial barriers to try and narrow it."

May Simone Biles continue to wear Goldie proudly, and may gymnastics' governing bodies finally catch up to her.

park skateboarding were Japan's Misugo Okamoto (fifteen), Britain's Sky Brown (thirteen, who took bronze) and Japan's Kokona Hiraki (twelve, who took silver).

The future looks like twin sisters Jocelyne Lamoureux-Davidson and Monique Lamoureux-Morando, gold Olympic medalists on the US Women's hockey team. In 2021 they published *Dare to Make History*, about their path to that gold medal. They share their story of growing up on a hockey rink, but the sisters also detail how they had to fight USA Hockey for more equitable treatment of their team. They were willing to boycott the 2017 World Championships (and potentially the 2018 Winter Olympics) to make their points about equity. Their fight—and their victory—created a changed landscape for future girls and women who play hockey.

Lamoureux-Morando says, "Our battle for gender equity in hockey had always been focused on the next generation of girls. We wanted to make sure that they would not face the same barriers that we had—that they knew the times were changing in education, sports, and the workplace."

**Lamoureux-Davidson and Lamoureux-Morando (*left to right*) won Olympic gold at the PyeongChang 2018 Olympic Games.**

The future looks like Sarah Thomas, the first female referee in NFL history to officiate the Super Bowl. She was the down judge in Super Bowl LV, played in February 2021. Thomas is the first full-time woman referee in the NFL and was hired in 2015. She played softball in high school and had a basketball scholarship to the University of Mobile, setting records while she was there. Her brothers played football, so she understood the game early, and she was a referee in college football before she moved to the NFL. The term "down judge" was created to refer to Thomas, because the position had previously been referred to as "head linesman." The name change for the position had been considered before her hiring, but the NFL wanted the gender-neutral name to encourage other women to apply as a referee, as well as to recognize Thomas in her position.

In addition to her historic Super Bowl appearance, Thomas was the first woman to officiate a major college football game and the first to officiate a bowl game.

The future looks like Thomas's counterparts in other professional sports: Natalie Sago and Jenna Schroeder, who were two of the three referees in the January 2021 NBA game between the Orlando Magic and the Charlotte Hornets. It was the first NBA game with two women officials. The NBA has five full-time women referees. In Major League Soccer, Kathryn Nesbitt was the first woman to officiate a championships game for the MLS in December 2020. Tori Penso was the first female official to be the head referee in a game in the MLS—in September 2020, twenty years after Sandy Hunt

# THE G. O. A. T. OF ADVOCACY IN SPORTS: BILLIE JEAN KING

No female athlete has done more to advance equity and equality in women's sports than Billie Jean King. Her tennis career is legendary—including her Battle of the Sexes match with Bobby Riggs in 1973, which she won—but her advocacy has set many precedents for the success of female players everywhere.

According to her website, King first experienced gender discrimination at the age of twelve, in 1955, at the Los Angeles Tennis Club. She was barred from a photo because she'd chosen to wear tennis shorts rather than a tennis skirt. When she became a professional tennis player, her monetary prizes for winning tournaments were less than men's prizes, and she fought hard to even out the prize money. King knew she had to maintain her top seed both to advance her career *and* to continue to fight—she knew she'd only be listened to if she was the best in her game. King cofounded World Team Tennis—the only professional coed sports league—in 1974, the same year she started *womenSports* magazine and the Women's Sports Foundation. Forty years later, she founded the Billie Jean King Leadership Initiative.

Outsports, a website that covers LGBTQIA+ athletes in all sports, argues that the third most important moment in LGBTQIA+ sports was Billie Jean King's outing in 1981. King was married to a man but was named in a lawsuit by her female partner, asking for monetary support. All of King's sponsors dropped her within twenty-four hours (an estimated $2 million loss in 1981 dollars, or approximately $6.08 million today). King had a homophobic family as well—she was finally able to speak to them honestly about being gay when she was fifty-one. She has been with partner Ilana Kloss, another professional tennis player and her previous doubles partner, since 1987.

King was awarded the Arthur Ashe Courage Award in 1999. Ashe was a Black professional tennis player, and the award is given to individuals in sports who continue Ashe's fight for racial equity. King was also awarded the Presidential Medal of Freedom in August 2009 by Obama, the first athlete to receive the honor. She was asked by Obama to head the US Olympic delegation to Sochi, Russia, for the 2014 Winter Olympics—as a gay woman, the appointment was crucially important because of Russia's harsh anti-LGBTQIA+ stance—but she was only able to attend the closing ceremonies because of a family member's illness.

**King lofts her trophy after winning all three sets in the Battle of the Sexes.**

King was the top athlete in *Sports Illustrated*'s list of "The Unrelenting"—"Our list of the most powerful, most influential and most outstanding women in sports right now." She is the oldest woman on the list, thus proving King has been fighting for equity and equality for her entire career.

The article about the list begins with something King said in 1970, as she was fighting for women to have equal prize money in tournaments: "Everyone thinks women should be thrilled when we get crumbs, and I want women to have the cake, the icing, and the cherry on top, too."

refereed a game in May 2000. During the 2020 season, Major League Soccer had nine women officials in its games.

The future looks like Adrianna Lobitz, a twenty-five-year-old master's student at the University of Minnesota who umpires women's fastpitch softball. She plans to umpire at the top of her field—those opportunities include the World Series for NCAA Division I games, the National Pro Fastpitch League, and the Olympics. Lobitz knows the field is dominated by men, but she's not intimidated: "It's incredibly important for women to officiate a women's game, and it's very special to have all women on the field. We don't need a man to tell us what to do, and we can work together to play the game. I still get to participate in the sport I love, but with a different angle—an important angle, because I get to preserve the integrity of the game."

Lobitz is deeply committed to bringing young women into umpiring: "It's important to me, professionally, to bring those young girls up in our game. If you can make it past the first two years of your work, you can really grow. I've had the best mentors, and not a lot of women are in the field. Women supporting women is a huge aspect of growing women officials."

The future looks like Fair Play for Girls in Sports, an organization in San Francisco, California, dedicated to making sure girls "regardless of race, income, and geography—receive equal opportunities, treatment, and benefits in athletics offered by schools and parks and recreation programs." The program was created by Legal Aid at Work, which enforces and expands the civil rights and employment of low-wage workers. Fair Play for Girls in Sports makes sure that the California gender equity legislation for parks and recreation athletics is upheld and utilized. According to its website, Black female athletes are more likely to graduate from college and Latina females who play sports will graduate from high school and attend college more often than their nonathletic peers.

The past, present, and future look like the Women's Sports Foundation, established by Billie Jean King in 1974 to encourage girls'

# TEAM USA'S WOMEN ATHLETES AT THE 2020 TOKYO OLYMPICS AND PARALYMPICS

US women athletes enjoyed immense success at the 2020 Tokyo Olympics and Paralympics. The United States won a total of 112 medals at the Olympics, and 66 of those medals were won by women. If the US women were their own country, they'd have placed fourth in the overall medal count and won more gold medals than women athletes from any other country. Women have led the medal count for four consecutive Summer Olympics and outnumbered men for three consecutive Summer Olympics.

The Paralympic women athletes also led Team USA, with 64 total (and 23 gold) medals brought home by women Paralympians. That total was 61.5 percent of US Paralympic medals and 62 percent of US Paralympic gold medals. The 2020 Tokyo Paralympics was the first Paralympics where Team USA had more women athletes than men (121 to 113).

These are other highlights from the 2020 Olympics and Paralympics:

- Runner Allyson Felix became the most decorated US track athlete, with eleven total medals to her name (two from Tokyo). Previously, that honor had been held by track star Carl Lewis.

- Dawn Staley became the first woman to earn gold medals as both a player and a coach. Staley has three gold medals as a US women's basketball player, two as an assistant coach, and one as the head coach. She is also the first Black head woman coach to win a gold medal.

- Basketball legend and gold medalist (1984) Pamela McGee and her son, JaVale, became the first mother-son duo to win gold Olympic medals.

- Two non-binary Paralympians won medals in their events: Robyn Lambird, an Australian wheelchair racer, won a bronze medal in the Women's 100-meter T34, and Australian Maz Strong won a bronze medal in shot put F33. The classifications T34 and F33 are sport classifications for athletes with disabilities, related to movement and strength.

- New Zealand weightlifter Laurel Hubbard and Canadian midfield soccer player Quinn (who identifies as non-binary) were the first two openly transgender athletes to compete at an Olympics.

and women's participation in sports at all levels. Their mission is "to advance the lives of women and girls through sports and physical activity." More specifically, "We provide financial fuel to aspiring champion athletes. We fund groundbreaking research. We educate. We advocate. And we help communities get girls active." They have programs and scholarships to girls' activity programs run through the community, college athletes striving to take their sports to the professional or Olympic level, women transitioning out of sports careers, women who want to coach and scout in football, students who want to play sports in college, and women who want to be physical education teachers.

Hundreds of other small sports organizations also do this work, but the Women's Sports Foundation appears to be the first and oldest organization dedicated to women and girls in sports.

The future looks like all girls having the opportunity to play the sport of their choice and to be supported in that choice—and having those sports funded and equipped equitably. It's trans girls and women being fully supported as members of women's sports teams. It's men's coaches, players, and owners standing up to the sexism and discrimination faced by women athletes.

The future looks like those girls on their soccer team's bench. It's those girls knowing they can play soccer and receive equal treatment from their club managers, as can their daughters someday. If these girls go on to college sports, they know their college athletic careers will be supported financially and materially in the same ways the men's teams are.

The future for women's sports looks bright. The future of sports will be more equitable for all if we put in the work. Olympic and professional hockey player Monique Lamoureux-Morando said, "Knowing that girls have traditionally been told they are less than, we want to be examples for girls everywhere that they can be more than—more than ever before . . . you don't ever have to think in terms of limitations. You can think of dreaming big. . . . Like those who paved the way for us, we're here so you can dare yourself to make history."

# GLOSSARY

**CIVIL RIGHTS ACT OF 1964:** a US law that "prohibits discrimination on the basis of race, color, religion, sex, or national origin," The law also "forbade discrimination on the basis of sex, as well as race, in hiring, promoting and firing," along with forbidding "discrimination in public accommodations and federally funded programs."

**EEOC:** the US Equal Employment Opportunity Commission takes responsibility for "enforcing federal laws that make it illegal to discriminate against a job applicant or an employee because of the person's race, color, religion, sex (including pregnancy, transgender status, and sexual orientation), national origin, age (40 or older), disability or genetic information." Title IX violations in workplaces with more than fifteen employers would involve the EEOC.

**FEMINISM:** advocating for the equality and equity of all humans, usually as advocating for women's rights in politics, society, and the economy

**INTERSECTIONALITY:** having more than one historically excluded identity that can compound the discrimination we experience

**NON-BINARY:** gender identities that are outside the binary (woman/man); also called genderqueer. For more information, see https://transequality.org/issues/resources/understanding-non-binary-people-how-to-be-respectful-and-supportive.

**SEX ASSIGNED AT BIRTH:** a label of male or female given at birth based on medical factors and entered on a birth certificate

**SEXISM:** prejudice or discrimination based on sex gender: the behavioral, cultural, or psychological traits of our identities. Gender can refer to traits typical of men and women, but some genders do not follow that binary. Gender can relate to identity, or it can relate to presentation.

**TRANSGENDER:** a person whose gender is different from the one assigned at birth

# SOURCE NOTES

6 Gentry Estes, "History Found Vanderbilt Football's Sarah Fuller, and It Turns Out She Was Perfect for It," *Nashville Tennessean*, November 28, 2020, https://www.tennessean.com/story/sports/college/vanderbilt/2020/11/28/sarah-fuller-vanderbilt-football-kickoff-first-woman-power-five-game/6450403002/.

7 Daisy, "Equality and Equity," *Social Change UK*, March 29, 2019, https://social-change.co.uk/blog/2019-03-29-equality-and-equity.

7 Jesse Newell, "LSU Banned Les Miles from 1-on-1 Contact with Female Students after 2013 Investigation," *Kansas City Star*, March 4, 2021, https://www.kansascity.com/sports/college/big-12/university-of-kansas/article249697288.html.

8 Lindsay Gibbs, "What, Disney???," Power Plays, March 3, 2021, https://www.powerplays.news/p/what-disney.

8 Gibbs.

9 Jeremy Bergman, "Toni Harris Is First Female Skill-Position Player to Sign

LOI," NFL.com, February 28, 2019, https://www.nfl.com/news/toni-harris
-is-first-female-skill-position-player-to-sign-loi-0ap3000001019418.

11   "History of Feminism," ThoughtCo., accessed February 20, 2021, https://
www.thoughtco.com/history-of-feminism-4133259.

12–13   Melina Lobitz, interview with the author, January 2021.

14   Billie Jean King, "Title IX," BillieJeanKing.com, accessed November 12, 2021,
https://www.billiejeanking.com/equality/title-ix/.

16   Jemima McEvoy, "Rand Paul Repeatedly Questions Education Nominee on
'Boys Competing with Girls' in Sports," *Forbes*, February 3, 2021, https://
www.forbes.com/sites/jemimamcevoy/2021/02/03/rand-paul-repeatedly
-questions-education-nominee-on-boys-competing-with-girls-in-sports/?sh
=7ff4f1da4031.

17   "Executive Order on Preventing and Combating Discrimination on the Basis
of Gender Identity or Sexual Orientation," Whitehouse.gov, January 20, 2021,
https://www.whitehouse.gov/briefing-room/presidential-actions/2021/01/20
/executive-order-preventing-and-combating-discrimination-on-basis-of-gender
-identity-or-sexual-orientation/.

18   Tony Maglio, "Australian Open Viewers Rip Chris Evert for Call of Serena
Williams Match: 'The Face of Misogynoir,'" The Wrap, February 18, 2021,
https://www.thewrap.com/chris-evert-serena-williams-drama-criticism
-australian-open-espn/.

18   "2018 US Open Highlights: Serena Williams' Dispute Overshadows Naomi
Osaka's Final Win," *ESPN*, September 8, 2018, https://www.youtube.com
/watch?v=uiBrForlj-k.

19   Crystal Fleming, "Opinion: Serena Williams: The Greatest Player of All
Time and a Classic Case of Misogynoir," *Time*, September 13, 2018, https://
www.newsweek.com/serena-williams-greatest-player-all-time-and-classic
-case-misogynoir-opinion-1119510.

19   Anne Branigin, "Serena Williams Fans Are Upset with This ESPN Analyst's
'Racially Coded' Commentary. It Isn't the First Time," Lily, February 18,
2021, https://www.thelily.com/serena-williams-fans-are-upset-with-this-espn
-analysts-racially-coded-commentary-it-isnt-the-first-time/.

23   "Title IX and Sex Discrimination," US Department of Education, April 2015,
https://www2.ed.gov/about/offices/list/ocr/docs/tix_dis.html.

26   Theresa A. Walton, "Framing Title IX: Conceptual Metaphors at Work,"
*Gender Relations in Sport*, ed. E. A. Roper (Boston: Sense, 2013), 106.

28   "What Is the NCAA?," NCAA.org, accessed February 6, 2021, https://
www.ncaa.org/about/resources/media-center/ncaa-101/what-ncaa.

29   Kaye Hart and Carol Oglesby, "AIAW Advocates Resist 'Sub'merger with
NCAA," Athletic Business, March 1979, https://www.athleticbusiness.com
/college/aiaw-advocates-resist-sub-merger-with-ncaa.html.

30   "Our Work," Women's Liberation Front, accessed January 29, 2021, https://
www.womensliberationfront.org/our-work.

31 Katie Barnes, "How Title IX Expanded to Protect LGBT Students," ABC News, January 17, 2017, https://abcnews.go.com/Sports/title-ix-expanded -protect-lgbt-students/story?id=44832919.

31, 34 "US Departments of Justice and Education Release Joint Guidance to Ensure the Civil Rights of Transgender Students," US Department of Justice, May 13, 2016, https://www.justice.gov/opa/pr/us-departments-justice-and -education-release-joint-guidance-help-schools-ensure-civil-rights.

33 Karen Given, "From the 'Jockbra' to Brandi Chastain: The History of the Sports Bra," WBUR, February 24, 2017, https://www.wbur.org/onlyagame /2017/02/24/sports-bra-lisa-lindahl.

36 "Executive Order," Whitehouse.gov.

40–41 Kathrine Switzer, "The Real Story of Kathrine Switzer's 1967 Boston Marathon," kathrineswitzer.com, accessed February 13, 2021, https:// kathrineswitzer.com/1967-boston-marathon-the-real-story/.

41 Switzer.

42 Melina Lobitz, interview with the author, January 25, 2021.

44 Carrie N. Baker, "Athletes Win First Round in Title IX Challenge to Cuts to Women's Sports," Ms., January 12, 2021, https://msmagazine.com/2021/01 /12/athletes-title-ix-lawsuit-university-iowa-womens-sports/.

44 Lindsey Peterson, "University of Minnesota Cutting Three Men's Sports Due to COVID," WCCO, September 10, 2020, https://www.radio.com/ wccoradio/articles/news/university-of-minnesota-cutting-three-mens-sports -due-covid.

45 Elizabeth Sharrow, "Pitting Men's and Women's Sports against Each Other at the U Is Wrong," Minneapolis Star Tribune, December 8, 2020, https:// www.startribune.com/pitting-men-s-and-women-s-sports-against-each-other -at-the-u-is-wrong/573336981/?refresh=true.

45 Carrie N. Baker, "Athletes Win First Round in Title IX Challenge to Cuts to Women's Sports," Ms., January 12, 2021, https://msmagazine.com/2021/01 /12/athletes-title-ix-lawsuit-university-iowa-womens-sports/.

45 Carrie N. Baker, "College Students Are Filing Record Number of Lawsuits to Fight Sex Discrimination in Athletics," Ms., January 28, 2021, https:// msmagazine.com/2021/01/28/title-ix-college-students-lawsuits-fight-sex -discrimination-women-sports/.

46 Baker.

47 Andrew Das, "U.S. Women's Soccer Team Sues U.S. Soccer for Gender Discrimination," New York Times, March 8, 2019, https://www.nytimes.com /2019/03/08/sports/womens-soccer-team-lawsuit-gender-discrimination.html

48 Daniel Politi, "Crowd in Stadium Starts Chanting 'Equal Pay' after U.S. Women's Team Wins World Cup," Slate, July 7, 2019, https://slate.com/news -and-politics/2019/07/crowd-stadium-chants-equal-pay-womens-team-wins -world-cup.html.

49 Emma Carmichael, "Megan Rapinoe and Sue Bird Are Goals," *GQ,* February 9, 2021, https://www.gq.com/story/megan-rapinoe-sue-bird-march-modern-lovers-cover.

50 Julie Compton, "Photo Series Explores 'Sexploitation' in Athletic Uniforms," NBC News, August 22, 2016, https://www.nbcnews.com/feature/nbc-out/photo-series-explores-sexploitation-athletic-uniforms-n635781.

50 Ben Baker-Katz and Hailey Fine, "Women's Sports Uniforms Are Blatantly Sexist," *Evanston (IL) Evanstonian*, April 26, 2019, https://www.evanstonian.net/sports/2019/04/26/womens-sports-uniforms-are-blatantly-sexist/.

51 Baker-Katz and Fine.

51 Des Biehler, "Wearing Unitards, German Gymnasts Promote Comfort, Take Stand against Sexualization," *Washington Post*, July 25, 2021, https://www.washingtonpost.com/sports/olympics/2021/07/25/german-gymnastics-unitards-olympics/.

52 Denise Grady, "Anatomy Does Not Determine Gender, Experts Say," *New York Times*, October 22, 2018, https://www.nytimes.com/2018/10/22/health/transgender-trump-biology.html.

52 Grady.

52 Simón(e) D. Sun, "Voices: Stop Using Phony Science to Justify Transphobia," *Scientific American*, June 13, 2019, https://blogs.scientificamerican.com/voices/stop-using-phony-science-to-justify-transphobia/.

54 Samantha Granville, "Namibian Teens Vow to Fight Olympics Testosterone Ban," BBC, July 7, 2021, https://www.bbc.com/news/world-africa-57748135.

55, 58 Rick Maese, "Stripped of Women's Records, Transgender Power Lifter Asks, 'Where Do We Draw the Line?,'" *Washington Post*, May 19, 2019, https://www.washingtonpost.com/sports/2019/05/16/stripped-womens-records-transgender-powerlifter-asks-where-do-we-draw-line/.

57 Minky Worden, "Swiss Court Upholds Regulations Biased against Women Athletes," Human Rights Watch, September 8, 2020, https://www.hrw.org/news/2020/09/08/caster-semenya-loses-appeal-equal-treatment#.

57 Worden.

58 Maese.

59 Juwan J. Holmes, "Georgia Considering 'a Panel of Three Physicians' to Evaluate Girls' Genitals for School Sports," LGBTQ Nation, February 13, 2021, https://www.lgbtqnation.com/2021/02/proposed-legislation-create-gender-panel-evaluating-athletes-georgia/.

59 Jessica Miles, "Transgender Student-Athletes Could Face Criminal Penalties in New Proposed Bill," KSTP, March 2, 2021, https://kstp.com/news/transgender-student-athletes-could-face-criminal-penalties-in-new-proposed-bill/6029528/.

59–60 Miles.

60 Miles.

60   "Executive Order," Whitehouse.gov.

60   Laura Meckler, "Cardona, Biden's Education Pick, Voices Support for Transgender Athletes," *Washington Post*, February 3, 2021, https:// www.washingtonpost.com/education/miguel-cardona-confirmation -hearing/2021/02/03/21d65be8-665c-11eb-8468-21bc48f07fe5_story.html.

61   "About Us," Women Sports Policy Working Group, accessed February 24, 2021, https://womenssportspolicy.org/about-us/#mission.

61   Britni de la Cretaz, "This Group Wants to Solve Sports' 'Transgender Problem.' There Are No Trans People in It," Them, February 4, 2021, https:// www.them.us/story/womens-sports-policy-working-group-anti-trans-athletes -martina-navratilova?fbclid=IwAR3YUb8TB0UCxt067dKLzttra-F07zqlRYd OdnEp2dFFWuUGbokBsQZQKfg.

61   La Cretaz.

62   Brynn Tannehill, Twitter thread, March 4, 2019, https://twitter.com /brynntannehill/status/1102568984556249090?lang=en.

62–63   Grace Walker, testimony to the Minnesota state legislature, April 5, 2021, https://www.senate.mn/committees/2021-2022/3106_Committee_on _Education_Finance_and_Policy/Grace%20Walker%20testimony%20 against%20SF%20960.pdf.

63   Katie McKellar, "Gov. Spencer Cox Says He Won't Sign Transgender Sports Bill as Now Written," *Deseret (UT) News*, February 18, 2021, https:// www.deseret.com/utah/2021/2/18/22289536/gov-spencer-cox-wont-sign -transgender-sports-bill-as-now-written-utah-legislature-2021-lgbt.

66   "American Notes: The Lady Ump," *Time*, January 24, 1972, http://content .time.com/time/subscriber/article/0,33009,905643,00.html.

68   Maggie Mertens, "Women's Soccer Is a Feminist Issue," *Atlantic*, June 5, 2015, https://www.theatlantic.com/entertainment/archive/2015/06/womens -soccer-is-a-feminist-issue/394865/.

69   Tucker Center for Research on Girls & Women in Sport, *Media Coverage and Female Athletes*, Minneapolis: TPT, December 1, 2013, https://www.cehd .umn.edu/tuckercenter/projects/mediacoverage.html.

70   Tucker Center for Research.

70   Lindsay Gibbs, "During the Pandemic, Mainstream Media Forgot about Women's Sports," Power Plays, June 18, 2020, https://www.powerplays.news /p/during-the-pandemic-mainstream-media.

71–72   Shira Springer, "7 Ways to Improve Coverage of Women's Sports," *Nieman Reports*, Winter 2019, https://niemanreports.org/articles/covering-womens-sports/.

72   "Why *Just* Women's Sports?," *Just Women's Sports*, accessed August 1, 2021, https://justwomenssports.com/about/.

72–73   Haley Rosen, "Why Just Women's Sports?," *Just Women's Sports*, December 9, 2019, https://justwomenssports.com/why-just-womens-sports/.

74   "NBC Olympics Enhances Accessibility for Olympic and Paralympic Games

in Tokyo," NBC Sports, July 22, 2021, https://nbcsportsgrouppressbox.com
/2021/07/22/nbc-olympics-enhances-accessibility-for-olympic-paralympic
-games-in-tokyo/.

75–76  Carmichael, "Megan Rapinoe and Sue Bird."

76   Chris Cwik, "WNBA Players Win Better Pay, Increased Marketing, and
      Family Benefits with New CBA," Yahoo Sports, January 14, 2020, https://
      sports.yahoo.com/wnba-players-win-better-pay-increased-marketing-and
      -more-family-benefits-with-new-cba-151309427.html.

78   Anya Alvarez, "I Thought the Main Issue in Women's Sports Was Equal Pay.
      I Was Wrong," *Guardian* (US edition), May 9, 2019, https://www.theguardian
      .com/sport/2019/may/09/i-thought-the-main-issue-in-womens-sports-was
      -equal-pay-i-was-wrong.

78   Laine Higgins, "Attendance at Women's College Basketball Games Is
      Surging," *Wall Street Journal*, March 5, 2020, https://www.wsj.com/articles
      /attendance-at-womens-college-basketball-games-is-surging-11583421714.

79   Cassandra Negley, "Why Olympians like Simone Biles and Breanna Stewart
      Have Bolted from Nike," Yahoo Sports, July 20, 2021, https://sports.yahoo
      .com/why-olympians-leave-nike-simone-biles-breanna-stewart-allyson-felix
      -045911863.html?guccounter=1&guce_referrer=aHR0cHM6Ly93d3cuZ
      29vZ2xlLmNvbS88&guce_referrer_sig=AQAAANkeKqK2rJBIoMSQsIkoYA5
      _3SpNpmGuVIKnCpNiKJ69WuOTFRXv6fpylmuKNvuld-SKCzyOewbxe
      R0wHr2TW0A6hyo6i_EjMwHUvCbSSqoujCkeKtYRFB9MMWjKDk7
      _-nH_gCUPyDIC58HXGB1-QtNww5Bq1fuXbONAA6LDvxt7.

79   Negley.

79   Sean Gregory, "Exclusive: Allyson Felix Launches Her Own Shoe Company
      Two Years after Breaking Up with Nike," *Time*, June 23, 2021, https://time
      .com/6073949/allyson-felix-launching-saysh-shoes/.

80   Nancy Armour, "Opinion: Sedona Prince Has Left Her Mark on NCAA
      Tournament, Women's Sports," *USA Today*, March 29, 2021, https://
      www.usatoday.com/story/sports/columnist/nancy-armour/2021/03/29
      /ncaa-tournament-sedona-prince-impact-women-goes-beyond-oregon
      /7042248002/.

80   David Moye, "Basketball Coach Slams NCAA's Treatment of Women. In Brutal
      Thank-You Note," HuffPost, March 23, 2021, https://www.huffpost.com/entry
      /nell-fortner-ncaa-thank-you-note_n_605a1c57c5b6d6c2a2aace38?fbclid
      =IwAR27uaPxmGovWO1g4NTwLS-xgNDMjKArbYIY-Pw0JEDYfBiQkwje
      _HsrpG8.

81   "Report: N.C.A.A. Prioritized Men's Basketball 'Over Everything Else,'"
      *New York Times*, August 3, 2021, https://www.nytimes.com/2021/08/03
      /sports/ncaabasketball/ncaa-gender-equity-investigation.html.

83   *#RespectHerGame Report*, Representation Project, August 3, 2021, https://
      therepproject.org/wp-content/uploads/2021/08/Respect-Her-Game-Report.pdf.

83   Brian C. Bell, "The Olympics and NBC Failed Alana Smith and the

Non-binary Community," Outsports, July 27, 2021, https://www.outsports .com/olympics/2021/7/26/22594536/alana-smith-nbc-bbc-tsn-non-binary -skateboarding-lgbtq.

85  "Empower Women through Sports," Global Sports Mentoring, accessed November 16, 2021, https://globalsportsmentoring.org/empower-women -through-sports/.

86  Laura Burton and Nicole M. LaVoi, "The War on Women Coaches," *Conversation*, June 4, 2019, https://theconversation.com/the-war-on-women -coaches-116643.

86  MM, interview with the author, June 2021.

86  Lobitz, interview.

87  Burton and LaVoi, "The War."

88  Becky Silva, "Best Practice Guides: Supporting Female Athletes," Squash and Education Alliance, July 2018, https://squashandeducation.org/wp-content /uploads/2018/07/Best-Practices-Female-Athletes.pdf.

89  Emily Iannaconi, "Washington Football Team Harassment Allegations Have Women in Sports Wondering, 'Is This Worth It?,'" *Forbes*, September 7, 2020, https://www.forbes.com/sites/emilyiannaconi/2020/09/07/the-mistreatment -of-women-by-the-washington-football-team-has-females-in-sports-wondering -is-this-worth-it/?sh=1b9da6b28c5e.

90  "Kobe Bryant and His Impact on Women's Sports," Positive Coaching Alliance, February 5, 2020, https://positivecoach.org/the-pca-blog/kobe -bryant-and-his-impact-on-women-s-sports/.

90  Kobe Bryant, "Kobe Bryant on LeBron, Lakers & Coaching His Daughter," *Jimmy Kimmel Live*, October 24, 2018, https://www.youtube.com/watch ?v=UUVubfIY2ns.

91  W. Brad Johnson and David G. Smith, "How Men Can Confront Other Men about Sexist Behavior," *Harvard Business Review*, October 16, 2020, https:// hbr.org/2020/10/how-men-can-confront-other-men-about-sexist-behavior.

91  Jerry Brewer, "Our Sports Need a Healthier Version of Masculinity, and Men Need to Create It," *Washington Post*, February 22, 2021, https:// www.washingtonpost.com/sports/2021/02/22/toxic-masculinity-sports -sexism-don-mcpherson/.

91  Brewer.

92–93  Coach M, interview with the author, February 26, 2021.

95  William Broussard, interview with the author, March 2 and 4, 2021.

95  Liz Elting, "Standing Up: What Men Can Do to Counter Systemic Sexism in the Office," *Forbes*, September 26, 2019, https://www.forbes.com/sites /lizelting/2019/09/26/standing-up-what-men-can-do-to-counter-systemic -sexism-in-the-office/?sh=22ada11d4b88.

96  Samantha Brodsky, "Simone Biles Says Celebrating Her Successes Isn't Cocky: 'The Facts Are Literally on Paper,'" PopSugar, October 17, 2019,

https://www.popsugar.com/fitness/simone-biles-interview-worlds-on-women-celebrating-success-46758371.

97–98 Marcela Howell, "Simone Biles, Naomi Osaka, and the Justice in Prioritizing Black Women's Mental Health," Rewire News Group, August 2, 2021, https://rewirenewsgroup.com/article/2021/08/02/simone-biles-naomi-osaka-and-the-justice-in-prioritizing-black-womens-mental-health/.

98 Naomi Osaka, "It's OK Not to Be OK," *Time*, July 8, 2021, https://time.com/6077128/naomi-osaka-essay-tokyo-olympics/.

99 James Pollard, "Watch Team USA's Suni Lee Discuss Gold-Medal Win," NBC New York, July 30, 2021, https://www.nbcnewyork.com/news/sports/tokyo-summer-olympics/watch-team-usas-suni-lee-discuss-gold-medal-win/3187837/.

100 Megan DiTrolio, "Simone Biles on Her GOAT Leotard: Don't Be Ashamed of Being Great," *Marie Claire*, June 14, 2021, https://www.marieclaire.com/culture/a36698899/simone-biles-goat-leotard-interview-2021/.

100–101 Nancy Armour, "Opinion: Simone Biles Penalized for Having Skills Other Gymnasts Can't Pull Off," *USA Today*, October 4, 2019, https://www.usatoday.com/story/sports/columnist/nancy-armour/2019/10/04/gymnastics-simon-biles-penalized-championships-being-too-good/3866255002/.

101 Nancy Armour, "Opinion: Punishing Simone Biles for Her Greatness Is Act of Foolishness by Gymnastics Officials," *USA Today*, May 23, 2021, https://www.usatoday.com/story/sports/columnist/nancy-armour/2021/05/23/simone-biles-gymnastics-officials-foolish-punishing-her-talent/5232267001/.

102 Joycelyne Lamoureux-Davidson and Monique Lamoureux-Morando, *Dare to Make History: Chasing a Dream and Fighting for Equity* (New York: Radius Book Group, 2021), 14.

105 *SI* staff, "The Unrelenting," *Sports Illustrated*, October 6, 2020, https://www.si.com/sports-illustrated/2020/10/06/the-unrelenting-women-in-sports-daily-cover. 105

106 Adrianna Lobitz, interview with the author, February 17, 2021.

106 Lobitz.

106 "Fair Play's Mission," Fair Play for Girls, accessed February 8, 2021, https://www.fairplayforgirlsinsports.org/.

108 Women's Sports Foundation, "WSF History," accessed August 25, 2021, https://www.womenssportsfoundation.org/who-we-are/.

108 Lamoureux-Davidson and Lamoureux-Morando, *Dare to Make History*, 22.

109 "Legal Highlight: The Civil Rights Act of 1964," US Department of Labor, accessed August 4, 2021, https://www.dol.gov/agencies/oasam/civil-rights-center/statutes/civil-rights-act-of-1964.

109 "Overview," US Equal Employment Opportunity Commission, accessed August 4, 2021, https://www.eeoc.gov/overview.

# SELECTED BIBLIOGRAPHY

Gibbs, Lindsay. *Power Plays*. Accessed February 20, 2021. https://www.powerplays.news/.

Lamoureux-Davidson, Joycelyne, and Monique Lamoureux-Morando. *Dare to Make History: Chasing a Dream and Fighting for Equity*. New York: Radius Book Group, 2021.

*Media Coverage and Female Athletes*. Minneapolis: TPT and Tucker Center for Research on Girls & Women in Sport, 2013.

Messner, Michael A. *Taking the Field: Women, Men and Sport*. Minneapolis: University of Minnesota Press, 2002.

Staurowsky, Ellen J., Nicholas Watanabe, Joseph Cooper, Cheryl Cooky, Nancy Lough, Amanda Paule-Koba, Jennifer Pharr et al. *Chasing Equity: The Triumphs, Challenges, and Opportunities for Girls and Women in Sports*. New York: Women's Sports Foundation: 2020.

Steidinger, Joan. *Stand Up and Shout Out: Women's Fight for Equal Pay, Equal Rights, and Equal Opportunities in Sports*. Lanham, MD: Rowman and Littlefield, 2020.

Transathlete.com. Accessed February 20, 2021. https://www.transatlete.com.

# FURTHER INFORMATION

## BOOKS

King, Billie Jean: *All In: An Autobiography*. New York: Knopf, 2021.

Rapinoe, Megan, and Emma Brockes. *One Life*. New York: Penguin, 2020.

Switzer, Kathrine. *Marathon Woman: Running the Race to Revolutionize Women's Sports*. New York: Da Capo, 2007.

Tyus, Wyomia, and Elizabeth Terzakis. *Tigerbelle: The Wyomia Tyus Story*. Brooklyn, NY: Edge of Sports, 2018.

## WEBSITES

Athlete Ally
> https://www.athleteally.org/
> Athlete Ally works to end homophobia and transphobia in three ways: they educate athlete communities, work on changing sport policy through discussions with legislative bodies including the federal government, and advocate for LGBTQIA+ rights.

ThoughtCo.
> https://www.thoughtco.com
> ThoughtCo. is a reference website with expert-created educational content about feminism, equity, and women's issues.

Transgender Athletes Amicus Brief
> https://www.aclu.org/legal-document/transgender-athletes-amicus-brief
> Read the full text of the amicus brief filed to support transgender girls in Idaho who want to play sports in their gender identity.

Women's Sports Foundation
> https://www.womenssportsfoundation.org
> The Women's Sports Foundation mentors, conducts research about, and provides scholarships for girls and women in sports.

# INDEX

## ACKNOWLEDGMENTS

The author wishes to thank the individuals who shared personal viewpoints about Title IX and women's athletics, including Adrianna Lobitz, Melina Lobitz, Coach M, MM, Dr. William Broussard, Grace Walker and her father, and Jennifer Cardone.

## PHOTO ACKNOWLEDGMENTS

Image credits: AP Photo/L.G. Patterson, p. 6; Dean Mouhtaropoulos/Getty Images, p. 7; AP Photo/Ben Liebenberg, p. 9; AP Photo/Yoshikazu Tsuno/Pool Photo, p. 14; AP Photo/Seth Wenig, p. 18; AP Photo/Press Association, p. 19; Popperfoto/Getty Images, pp. 21, 22; Library of Congress (LC-DIG-ppmsca-37810), p. 24; National Collegiate Athletic Association, p. 26; 609design.com/Wikimedia Commons, p. 29; Further information on gender equity provided by NCAA.org, p. 33; AP Photo/Carolyn Kaster, p. 34; Alex Wong/Getty Images, p. 37; Paul J. Connell/The Boston Globe/Getty Images, p. 40; Ira L. Black/Corbis/Getty Images, p. 49; LIONEL BONAVENTURE/AFP/Getty Images, p. 51; Peter Sonksen OBE MD FRCP FFSEM(UK), p. 53; Ryan Pierse/Getty Images, p. 54; Parker Michels-Boyce for The Washington Post/Getty Images, p. 55; AP Photo/Jae C. Hong, p. 57; Fred Morgan/NY Daily News Archive/Getty Images, p. 67; Marco Ciccolella/Shutterstock.com, p. 71; Leon Halip/Getty Images, p. 77; AP Photo/Eric Gay, p. 80; Patrick Smith/Getty Images, p. 83; Michael Reaves/Getty Images, p. 87; Chip Somodevilla/Getty Images, p. 89; Allen Berezovsky/Getty Images, p. 90; Al Bello/Getty Images, p. 97; The Asahi Shimbun/Getty Images, p. 99; Emilee Chinn/Getty Images, p. 101; Harry How/Getty Images, p. 102; AP Photo/Ben Liebenberg, p. 103; Jerry Cooke /Sports Illustrated/AP Photo, p. 105. Cover and jacket images: Tickstylestock/Shutterstock.com; OSTILL is Franck Camhi/Shutterstock.com.